Human Rights and U.S. Human Rights Policy

Theoretical Approaches and Some Perspectives on Latin America

Edited by Howard J. Wiarda

Mark Falcoff Edward A. Olsen

Jeane J. Kirkpatrick Richard Schifter

Michael Novak Howard J. Wiarda

American Enterprise Institute for Public Policy Research
Washington and London

Howard J. Wiarda is professor of political science at the University of Massachusetts and director of the Center for Hemispheric Studies at the American Enterprise Institute.

Library of Congress Cataloging in Publication Data
Main entry under title:

Human rights and United States human rights policy.

    (AEI studies ; 351)
    1. Civil rights—Addresses, essays, lectures.
2. Civil rights—Latin America—Addresses, essays,
lectures. 3. United States—Foreign relations—
Addresses, essays, lectures. I. Wiarda, Howard J.,
1939– . II. Series.
JC571.H7689   323.4   82–1636
ISBN 0–8447–3481–0   AACR2

AEI Studies 351

Printed in the United States of America

Contents

Contributors

HOWARD J. WIARDA is professor of political science at the University of Massachusetts and director of the Center for Hemispheric Studies at AEI. He has been a visiting professor of political science at MIT and visiting scholar at the Center for International Affairs, Harvard University. His most recent books include *Latin American Politics and Development, The Continuing Struggle for Democracy in Latin America, Corporatism and National Development in Latin America, The Dominican Republic: Caribbean Crucible, Politics and Social Change in Latin America,* and *The Labor Relations Systems of Southern Europe.*

MARK FALCOFF is resident fellow of the Center for Hemispheric Studies, American Enterprise Institute. He has taught at the Universities of Illinois, Oregon, and California (Los Angeles) and is a former fellow of the Hoover Institution on War, Revolution and Peace, Stanford University. He has written (with Fredrick B. Pike) *The Spanish Civil War, 1936–39: American Hemispheric Perspectives,* published by University of Nebraska Press.

JEANE J. KIRKPATRICK is the United States permanent representative to the United Nations. Ambassador Kirkpatrick is on leave as resident scholar at AEI and as Leavey University Professor and professor of government at Georgetown University. Her books include *The New Presidential Elite, Leader and Vanguard in Mass Society,* and *Dismantling the Parties: Reflections on Party Reform and Party Decomposition.*

MICHAEL NOVAK is a resident scholar at AEI and adjunct professor of religion at Syracuse University. He served as the special representative and chief of the United States delegation to the United Nations Human Rights Commission. He is a well-known commentator and writer on social, political, and theological issues; his books include *The American Vision, Belief and Unbelief,* and *The Guns of Lattimer.*

EDWARD A. OLSEN is associate professor and coordinator of Asian-Pacific Studies in the National Security Affairs Department of the Naval Postgraduate School in Monterey, California. From 1975 to 1980 he was an intelligence analyst at the Department of State, where he regularly reported on human rights. His research interests are focused on U.S.-Japanese and U.S.-Korean security relations.

RICHARD SCHIFTER, a practicing attorney in Washington, has served as president of the Maryland State Board of Education and chairman of the Maryland Values Education Commission. Along with Mr. Novak, he served on the U.S. delegation to the United Nations Human Rights Commission.

Introduction

HOWARD J. WIARDA

The debate over human rights and the place of human rights in United States foreign policy is hardly new. The literature on international relations is replete with discussions of the advisability of this country's following an ethical, as opposed to a realistic or pragmatic, foreign policy; that debate in turn is related to the persistent ideal of American exceptionalism, that with our New World origins and fresh start this country is and should be different from the Machiavellian Europeans in the pursuit of morality in its international affairs. National interest may have been consistently at the heart of our foreign policy pursuits, but that seemingly mundane and inglorious concern has been just as consistently covered over with the language of priorities presumably of a higher order: manifest destiny, freeing Cuba and Puerto Rico from the yoke of Spanish oppression, making the world safe for democracy, and now human rights. The ancient debate has been renewed in the struggle over human rights policy in the Carter and Reagan administrations and in the controversy over the appropriate stance of the United States, the priority that human rights should have in policy determinations, and the possibility of balancing U.S. considerations of human rights with other foreign policy objectives.

Latin America has been the special focus of human rights policy. The reasons for this are not entirely clear. Probably it has to do with the fact that we still harbor suspicions about the supposedly Catholic-inquisitorial character of Latin American society; probably with the fact that since Latin America is "Western" (as compared with Iran or Uganda, let us say), we expect more from it than from other areas; probably with the fact that we believe we can carry out foreign policy experiments in Latin America without fear of retribution or retaliation (as contrasted with what could be done in the Soviet Union). Whatever the reasons, it is a curious fact, one that may well be worth exploring further, that Latin America has attracted more than its share of human rights attention. It is for this reason that in the present collection we have combined some general and conceptual essays on human rights

1

and human rights policy with a series of especially provocative statements particularly focused on Latin America.

It should be clear by now that to be critical of the Carter administration's human rights policy, as most of these essays are, is not to assume a posture of being against human rights. Indeed, the authors included here are all fervent believers in human rights, seeing respect for human rights as crucial to our existence and purpose as a nation and worth fighting and struggling for. What these authors object to is certainly not a strong human rights strategy, but rather the human rights policy of a particular administration that was frequently fumbling, uninformed, undiscriminating, unsophisticated, unaware of or unsympathetic to national and cultural differences, unable to distinguish between the totalitarian behemoth and the generally milder forms of authoritarian repression, unwilling to condemn the violations of leftist regimes as strongly as rightist ones, and, in the end, unable to see that the blunt and blatant tactics it used led as often to further repression as to the greater respect for human rights it ostensibly sought. Our purpose is to present this critique honestly and completely, in the original words of a number of the key people involved in the debate and without the caricature, distortion, misrepresentation (sometimes purposeful), or parody to which these views were sometimes subjected in the media.

The essays collected here call for a more refined, sophisticated, informed, sensitive, and even-handed human rights policy, but one that is no less forceful for being so. Clearly the appointment of Elliot Abrams as assistant secretary for human rights and humanitarian affairs and the issuance of a new position paper on human rights policy approved by the secretary of state and the president stating that "human rights is at the core of our foreign policy" provide strong indications of a continuing commitment to human rights. The tactics, strategies, and emphases may be somewhat different from those of the previous administration, but of the fact of our belief in and commitment to human rights there should be no doubt.

There are of course other points of view on human rights besides those presented here, and in its research work and publications AEI is committed to exploration of a diversity of perspectives. But for purposes of this volume we have thought it best to put together a more or less coherent and integrated collection of statements that argue some common themes from some related assumptions. That is not to say that all our authors are in complete agreement on all aspects of each other's essays; within a large and diverse research center such as AEI and on such an emotion-laden topic complete unanimity of views would probably be both hard to achieve and at odds with our individual research objectives. Rather, what the collection does is to bring together in a single volume some diverse essays, most of which have been published before but often in obscure and not immediately accessible places, essays organized around some common themes and now readily available as a more or less unified, clearly articulated, and consistent set of statements with important policy implications.

The first essay is the forceful and important statement "Dictatorships and Double Standards," by United Nations Ambassador Jeane Kirkpatrick. That essay, which had a significant part in shaping the Reagan administration's foreign policy, has been more often cited than read; it merits a careful and thorough reading. The second essay, by the editor, explores what democracy and human rights mean in Latin America, how this is different from the United States conception, and what these differences imply for policy. In the third essay attorney Richard Schifter presents a strong and vigorous statement of the United States position concerning human rights.

In the fourth essay Mark Falcoff offers the best treatment yet available of the celebrated case of the Argentine newspaperman and author Jacobo Timerman and significantly increases our understanding by analyzing the case within the Argentine context. Michael Novak's essay, "Human Rights and Whited Sepulchres," provides a well-stated critique of some of our earlier miscomprehensions and missteps in the human rights area.

Ambassador Kirkpatrick's second essay provides positive advice on how to establish a viable human rights policy and serves as a nice complement to her earlier critique. Finally, Edward A. Olsen offers a brief statement of advice on human rights policy, much of which has already been incorporated into the administration's program.

It is a provocative collection and one that should both clear away some of the confusion surrounding the human rights issue while also providing a basis for future discussion and policy.

Dictatorships and Double Standards

JEANE J. KIRKPATRICK

The failure of the Carter administration's foreign policy is now clear to everyone except its architects, and even they must entertain private doubts, from time to time, about a policy whose crowning achievement has been to lay the groundwork for a transfer of the Panama Canal from the United States to a swaggering Latin dictator of Castroite bent. In the thirty-odd months since the inauguration of Jimmy Carter as President there has occurred a dramatic Soviet military build-up, matched by the stagnation of American armed forces, and a dramatic extension of Soviet influence in the Horn of Africa, Afghanistan, Southern Africa, and the Caribbean, matched by a declining American position in all these areas. The U.S. has never tried so hard and failed so utterly to make and keep friends in the Third World.

As if this were not bad enough, in the current year the United States has suffered two other major blows—in Iran and Nicaragua—of large and strategic significance. In each country, the Carter administration not only failed to prevent the undesired outcome, it actively collaborated in the replacement of moderate autocrats friendly to American interests with less friendly autocrats of extremist persuasion. It is too soon to be certain about what kind of regime will ultimately emerge in either Iran or Nicaragua, but accumulating evidence suggests that things are as likely to get worse as to get better in both countries. The Sandinistas in Nicaragua appear to be as skillful in consolidating power as the Ayatollah Khomeini is inept, and leaders of both revolutions display an intolerance and arrogance that do not bode well for the peaceful sharing of power or the establishment of constitutional governments, especially since those leaders have made clear that they have no intention of seeking either.

NOTE: Reprinted from *Commentary*, November 1979, pp. 34–35, by permission. All rights reserved.

It is at least possible that the SALT debate may stimulate new scrutiny of the nation's strategic position and defense policy, but there are no signs that anyone is giving serious attention to this nation's role in Iranian and Nicaraguan developments—despite clear warnings that the U.S. is confronted with similar situations and options in El Salvador, Guatemala, Morocco, Zaire, and elsewhere. Yet no problem of American foreign policy is more urgent than that of formulating a morally and strategically acceptable, and politically realistic, program for dealing with non-democratic governments who are threatened by Soviet-sponsored subversion. In the absence of such a policy, we can expect that the same reflexes that guided Washington in Iran and Nicaragua will be permitted to determine American actions from Korea to Mexico—with the same disastrous effects on the U.S. strategic position. (That the administration has not called its policies in Iran and Nicaragua a failure—and probably does not consider them such—complicates the problem without changing its nature.)

There were, of course, significant differences in the relations between the United States and each of these countries during the past two or three decades. Oil, size, and proximity to the Soviet Union gave Iran greater economic and strategic import than any Central American "republic," and closer relations were cultivated with the Shah, his counselors, and family than with President Somoza, his advisers, and family. Relations with the Shah were probably also enhanced by our approval of his manifest determination to modernize Iran regardless of the effects of modernization on traditional social and cultural patterns (including those which enhanced his own authority and legitimacy). And, of course, the Shah was much better looking and altogether more dashing than Somoza; his private life was much more romantic, more interesting to the media, popular and otherwise. Therefore, more Americans were more aware of the Shah than of the equally tenacious Somoza.

But even though Iran was rich, blessed with a product the U.S. and its allies needed badly, and led by a handsome king, while Nicaragua was poor and rocked along under a long-tenure president of less striking aspect, there were many similarities between the two countries and our relations with them. Both these small nations were led by men who had not been selected by free elections, who recognized no duty to submit themselves to searching tests of popular acceptability. Both did tolerate limited opposition, including opposition newspapers and political parties, but both were also confronted by radical, violent opponents bent on social and political revolution. Both rulers, therefore, sometimes invoked martial law to arrest, imprison, exile, and occasionally, it was alleged, torture their opponents.

Both relied for public order on police forces whose personnel were said to be too harsh, too arbitrary, and too powerful. Each had what the American press termed "private armies," which is to say, armies pledging their allegiance to the ruler rather than the "constitution" or the "nation" or some other impersonal entity.

In short, both Somoza and the Shah were, in central ways, traditional rulers of semi-traditional societies. Although the Shah very badly wanted to create a technologically modern and powerful nation and Somoza tried hard to introduce modern agricultural methods, neither sought to reform his society in the light of any abstract idea of social justice or political virtue. Neither attempted to alter significantly the distribution of goods, status, or power (though the democratization of education and skills that accompanied modernization in Iran did result in some redistribution of money and power there).

Both Somoza and the Shah enjoyed long tenure, large personal fortunes (much of which were no doubt appropriated from general revenues), and good relations with the United States. The Shah and Somoza were not only anti-Communist, they were positively friendly to the U.S., sending their sons and others to be educated in our universities, voting with us in the United Nations, and regularly supporting American interests and positions even when these entailed personal and political cost. The embassies of both governments were active in Washington social life, and were frequented by powerful Americans who occupied major roles in this nation's diplomatic, military, and political life. And the Shah and Somoza themselves were both welcome in Washington, and had many American friends.

Though each of the rulers was from time to time criticized by American officials for violating civil and human rights, the fact that the people of Iran and Nicaragua only intermittently enjoyed the rights accorded to citizens in the Western democracies did not prevent successive administrations from granting—with the necessary approval of successive Congresses—both military and economic aid. In the case of both Iran and Nicaragua, tangible and intangible tokens of U.S. support continued until the regime became the object of a major attack by forces explicitly hostile to the United States.

But once an attack was launched by opponents bent on destruction, everything changed. The rise of serious, violent opposition in Iran and Nicaragua set in motion a succession of events which bore a suggestive resemblance to one another and a suggestive similarity to our behavior in China before the fall of Chiang Kai-shek, in Cuba before the triumph of Castro, in certain crucial periods of the Vietnamese war, and, and, more recently, in Angola. In each of these countries, the American effort to impose liberalization and democratization on a government confronted with violent internal opposition not only failed, but actually assisted the coming to power of new regimes in which ordinary people enjoy fewer freedoms and less personal security than under the previous autocracy—regimes, moreover, hostile to American interests and policies.

The pattern is familiar enough: an established autocracy with a record of friendship with the U.S. is attacked by insurgents, some of whose leaders have long ties to the Communist movement, and most of whose arms are of Soviet, Chinese, or Czechoslovak origin. The "Marxist" presence is ignored and/or minimized by American officials and by the elite media on the ground that U.S. support for the dictator gives the rebels little choice but to seek aid "elsewhere." Violence spreads and American officials wonder aloud about the viability of a regime that "lacks the support of its own people." The absence of an opposition party is deplored and civil-rights violations are reviewed. Liberal columnists question the morality of continuing aid to a "rightist dictatorsip" and provide assurances concerning the essential moderation of some insurgent leaders who "hope" for some sign that the U.S. will remember its own revolutionary origins. Requests for help from the beleaguered autocrat go unheeded, and the argument is increasingly voiced that ties should be established with rebel leaders "before it is too late." The President, delaying U.S. aid, appoints a special emissary who confirms the deterioration of the government position and its diminished capacity to control the situation and recommends various measures for "strengthening" and "liberalizing" the regime, all of which involve diluting its power.

The emissary's recommendations are presented in the context of a growing clamor for American disengagement on grounds that continued involvement confirms our status as an agent of imperialism, racism, and reaction; is inconsistent with support for human rights; alienates us from the "forces of democracy"; and threatens to put the U.S. once more on the side of history's "losers." This chorus is supplemented daily by interviews with returning missionaries and "reasonable" rebels.

As the situation worsens, the President assures the world that the U.S. desires only that the "people choose their own form of government"; he blocks delivery of all arms to the government and undertakes negotiations to establish a "broadly based" coalition headed by a "moderate" critic of the regime who, once elevated, will move quickly to seek a "political" settlement to the conflict. Should the incumbent autocrat prove resistant to American demands that he step aside, he will be readily overwhelmed by the military strength of his opponents, whose patrons will have continued to provide sophisticated arms and advisers at the same time the U.S. cuts off military sales. Should the incumbent be so demoralized as to agree to yield power, he will be replaced by a "moderate" of American selection. Only after the insurgents have refused the proffered political solution and anarchy has spread throughout the nation will it be noticed that the new head of government has no significant following, no experience at governing, and no talent for leadership. By then, military commanders, no longer bound by loyalty to the chief of state, will depose the faltering "moderate" in favor of a fanatic of their own choosing.

In either case, the U.S. will have been led by its own misunderstanding of the situation to assist actively in deposing an erstwhile friend and ally and installing a government hostile to American interests and policies in the world. At best we will have lost access to friendly territory. At worst the Soviets will have gained a new base. And everywhere our friends will have noted that the U.S. cannot be counted on in times of difficulty and our enemies will have observed that American support provides no security against the forward march of history.

No particular crisis conforms exactly with the sequence of events described above; there are always variations on the theme. In Iran, for example, the Carter administration—and the President himself— offered the ruler support for a longer time, though by December 1978 the President was acknowledging that he did not know if the Shah would survive, adding that the U.S. would not get "directly involved." Neither did the U.S. ever call publicly for the Shah's resignation. However, the President's special emissary, George Ball, "reportedly concluded that the Shah cannot hope to maintain total power and must now bargain with a moderate segment of the opposition . . ." and was "known to have discussed various alternatives that would effectively ease the Shah out of total power" (Washington *Post*, December 15, 1978). There is, furthermore, not much doubt that the U.S. assisted the Shah's departure and helped arrange the succession of Bakhtiar. In Iran, the Carter administration's commitment to nonintervention proved stronger than strategic considerations or national pride. What the rest of the world regarded as a stinging American defeat, the U.S. government saw as a matter to be settled by Iranians. "We personally prefer that the Shah maintain a major role in the goverment," the President acknowledged, "but that is a decision for the Iranian people to make."

Events in Nicaragua also departed from the scenario presented above both because the Cuban and Soviet roles were clearer and because U.S. officials were more intensely and publicly working against Somoza. After the Somoza regime had defeated the first wave of Sandinista violence, the U.S. ceased aid, imposed sanctions, and took other steps which undermined the status and the credibility of the government in domestic and foreign affairs. Between the murder of ABC correspondent Bill Stewart by a National Guardsman in early June and the Sandinista victory in late July, the U.S. State Department assigned a new ambassador who refused to submit his credentials to Somoza even though Somoza was still chief of state, and called for replacing the goverment with a "broadly based provisional government that would include representatives of Sandinista guerrillas." Americans were assured by Assistant Secretary of State Viron Vaky that "Nicaraguans and our democratic friends in Latin America have no intention of seeing Nicaragua turned into a second Cuba," even though the State Department knew that the top Sandinista leaders had close personal ties and were in continuing contact with Havana, and, more specifically, that a Cuban secret-police official, Julian López, was frequently present in the Sandinista headquarters and that Cuban military advisers were present in Sandinista ranks.

In a manner uncharacteristic of the Carter administration, which generally seems willing to negotiate anything with anyone anywhere, the U.S. government adopted an oddly uncompromising posture in dealing with Somoza. "No end to the crisis is possible," said Vaky, "that does not start with the departure of Somoza from power and the end of his regime. No negotiation, mediation, or compromise can be achieved any longer with a Somoza government. The solution can only begin with a sharp break from the past." Trying hard, we not only banned all American arms sales to the government of Nicaragua but pressured Israel, Guatemala, and others to do likewise—all in the name of insuring a "democratic" outcome. Finally, as the Sandinista leaders consolidated control over weapons and communications, banned opposition, and took off for Cuba, President Carter warned us against attributing this "evolutionary change" to "Cuban machinations" and assured the world that the U.S. desired only to "let the people of Nicaragua choose their own form of government."

Yet despite all the variations, the Carter administration brought to the crises in Iran and Nicaragua several common assumptions each of which played a major role in hastening the victory of even more repressive dictatorships than had been in place before. These were, first, the belief that there existed at the moment of crisis a democratic alternative to the incumbent government; second, the belief that the continuation of the status quo was not possible; third, the belief that any change, including the establishment of a government headed by self-styled Marxist revolutionaries, was preferable to the present government. Each of these beliefs was (and is) widely shared in the liberal community generally. Not one of them can withstand close scrutiny.

Although most governments in the world are, as they always have been, autocracies of one kind or another, no idea holds greater sway in the minds of educated Americans than the belief that it is possible to democratize governments, anytime, anywhere, under any circumstances. This notion is belied by an enormous body of evidence based on the experience of dozens of countries which have attempted with more or less (usually less) success to move from autocratic to democratic government. Many of the wisest political scientists of this and previous centuries agree that democratic institutions are especially difficult to establish and maintain—because they make heavy demands on all portions of a population and because they depend on complex social, cultural, and economic conditions.

Two or three decades ago, when Marxism enjoyed its greatest prestige among American intellectuals, it was the economic prerequisites of democracy that were emphasized by social scientists. Democracy, they argued, could function only in relatively rich societies with an advanced economy, a substantial middle class, and a literate population, but it could be expected to emerge more or less automatically whenever these conditions prevailed. Today, this picture seems grossly oversimplified. While it surely helps to have an economy strong enough to provide decent levels of well-being for all, and "open" enough to provide mobility and encourage achievement, a pluralistic society and the right kind of political culture—and time—are even more essential.

In his essay on *Representative Government*, John Stuart Mill identified three fundamental conditions which the Carter administration would do well to ponder. These are: "One, that the people should be willing to receive it [representative government]; two, that they should be willing and able to do what is necessary for its preservation; three, that they should be willing and able to fulfill the duties and discharge the functions which it imposes on them."

Fulfilling the duties and discharging the functions of representative government make heavy demands on leaders and citizens, demands for participation and restraint, for consensus and compromise. It is not necessary for all citizens to be avidly interested in politics

11

or well-informed about public affairs—although far more widespread interest and mobilization are needed than in autocracies. What *is* necessary is that a substantial number of citizens think of themselves as participants in society's decision-making and not simply as subjects bound by its laws. Moreover, leaders of all major sectors of the society must agree to pursue power only by legal means, must eschew (at least in principle) violence, theft, and fraud, and must accept defeat when necessary. They must also be skilled at finding and creating common ground among diverse points of view and interests, and correlatively willing to compromise on all but the most basic values.

In addition to an appropriate political culture, democratic government requires institutions strong enough to channel and contain conflict. Voluntary, non-official institutions are needed to articulate and aggregate diverse interests and opinions present in the society. Otherwise, the formal governmental institutions will not be able to translate popular demands into public policy.

In the relatively few places where they exist, democratic governments have come into being slowly, after extended prior experience with more limited forms of participation during which leaders have reluctantly grown accustomed to tolerating dissent and opposition, opponents have accepted the notion that they may defeat but not destroy incumbents, and people have become aware of government's effects on their lives and of their own possible effects on government. Decades, if not centuries, are normally required for people to acquire the necessary disciplines and habits. In Britain, the road from the Magna Carta to the Act of Settlement, to the great Reform Bills of 1832, 1867, and 1885, took seven centuries to traverse. American history gives no better grounds for believing that democracy comes easily, quickly, or for the asking. A war of independence, an unsuccessful constitution, a civil war, a long process of gradual enfranchisement marked our progress toward constitutional democratic government. The French path was still more difficult. Terror, dictatorship, monarchy, instability, and incompetence followed on the revolution that was to usher in a millennium of brotherhood. Only in the 20th century did the democratic principle finally gain wide acceptance in France and not until after World War II were the principles of order and democracy, popular sovereignty and authority, finally reconciled in institutions strong enough to contain conflicting currents of public opinion.

Although there is no instance of a revolutionary "socialist" or Communist society being democratized, right-wing autocracies do sometimes evolve into democracies—given time, propitious economic, social, and political circumstances, talented leaders, and a strong indigenous demand for representative government. Something of the kind is in progress on the Iberian peninsula and the first steps have been taken in Brazil. Something similar could conceivably have also occurred in Iran and Nicaragua if contestation and participation had been more gradually expanded.

But it seems clear that the architects of contemporary American foreign policy have little idea of how to go about encouraging the liberalization of an autocracy. In neither Nicaragua nor Iran did they realize that the only likely result of an effort to replace an incumbent autocrat with one of his moderate critics or a "broad-based coalition" would be to sap the foundations of the existing regime without moving the nation any closer to democracy. Yet this outcome was entirely predictable. Authority in traditional autocracies is transmitted through personal relations: from the ruler to his close associates (relatives, household members, personal friends) and from them to people to whom the associates are related by personal ties resembling their own relation to the ruler. The fabric of authority unravels quickly when the power and status of the man at the top are undermined or eliminated. The longer the autocrat has held power, and the more pervasive his personal influence, the more dependent a nation's institutions will be on him. Without him, the organized life of the society will collapse, like an arch from which the keystone has been removed. The blend of qualities that bound the Iranian army to the Shah or the national guard to Somoza is typical of the relationships—personal, hierarchical, non-transferable—that support a traditional autocracy. The speed with which armies collapse, bureaucracies abdicate, and social structures dissolve once the autocrat is removed frequently surprises American policy-makers and journalists accustomed to public institutions based on universalistic norms rather than particularistic relations.

The failure to understand these relations is one source of the failure of U.S. policy in this and previous administrations. There are others. In Iran and Nicaragua (as previously in Vietnam, Cuba, and China) Washington overestimated the political diversity of the opposition—especially the strength of "moderates" and "democrats" in the opposition movement; underestimated the strength and intransigence of radicals in the movement; and misestimated the nature and extent of American influence on both the government and the opposition.

Confusion concerning the character of the opposition, especially its intransigence and will to power, leads regularly to downplaying the amount of force required to counteract its violence. In neither Iran nor Nicaragua did the U.S. adequately appreciate the government's problem in maintaining order in a society confronted with an ideologically extreme opposition. Yet the presence of such groups was well known. The State Department's 1977 report on human rights described an Iran confronted

> with a small number of extreme rightist and leftist terrorists operating within the country. There is evidence that they have received substantial foreign support and training. . . [and] have been responsible for the murder of Iranian government officials and Americans. . . .

The same report characterized Somoza's opposition in the following terms:

> A guerrilla organization known as the Sandinista National Liberation Front (FSLN) seeks the violent overthrow of the government, and has received limited support from Cuba. The FSLN carried out an operation in Managua in December 1974, killing four people, taking several officials hostage, . . . since then, it continues to challenge civil authority in certain isolated regions.

In 1978, the State Department's report said that Sandinista violence was continuing—after the state of siege had been lifted by the Somoza government.

When U.S. policy-makers and large portions of the liberal press interpret insurgency as evidence of widespread popular discontent and a will to democracy, the scene is set for disaster. For if civil strife reflects a popular demand for democracy, it follows that a "liberalized" government will be more acceptable to "public opinion."

Thus, in the hope of strengthening a government, U.S. policy-makers are led, mistake after mistake, to impose measures almost certain to weaken its authority. Hurried efforts to force complex and unfamiliar political practices on societies lacking the requisite political culture, tradition, and social structures not only fail to produce desired outcomes; if they are undertaken at a time when the traditional regime is under attack, they actually facilitate the job of the insurgents.

Vietnam presumably taught us that the United States could not serve as the world's policeman; it should also have taught us the dangers of trying to be the world's midwife to democracy when the birth is scheduled to take place under conditions of guerrilla war.

If the administration's actions in Iran and Nicaragua reflect the pervasive and mistaken assumption that one can easily locate and impose democratic alternatives to incumbent autocracies, they also reflect the equally pervasive and equally flawed belief that change *per se* in such autocracies is inevitable, desirable, and in the American interest. It is this belief which induces the Carter administration to participate actively in the toppling of non-Communist autocracies while remaining passive in the face of Communist expansion.

At the time the Carter administration came into office it was widely reported that the President had assembled a team who shared a new approach to foreign policy and a new conception of the national interest. The principal elements of this new approach were said to be two: the conviction that the cold war was over, and the conviction that, this being the case, the U.S. should give priority to North-South problems and help less developed nations achieve their own destiny.

More is involved in these changes than originally meets the eye. For, unlikely as it may seem, the foreign policy of the Carter administration is guided by a relatively full-blown philosophy of history which includes, as philosophies of history always do, a theory of social change, or, as it is currently called, a doctrine of modernization. Like most other philosophies of history that have appeared in the West since the 18th century, the Carter administration's doctrine predicts progress (in the form of modernization for all societies) and a happy ending (in the form of a world community of developed, autonomous nations).

The administration's approach to foreign affairs was clearly fore-shadowed in Zbigniew Brzezinski's 1970 book on the U.S. role in the "technetronic era," *Between Two Ages*. In that book, Brzezinski showed that he had the imagination to look beyond the cold war to a brave new world of global politics and interdependence. To deal with that new world a new approach was said to be "evolving," which Brzezinski designated "rational humanism." In the new approach, the "pre-occupation" with "national supremacy" would give way to "global" perspectives, and international problems would be viewed as "human issues" rather than as "political confrontations." The traditional intellectual framework for dealing with foreign policy would have to be scrapped:

> Today, the old framework of international politics... with their spheres of influence, military alliances between nation states, the fiction of sovereignty, doctrinal conflicts arising from 19th-century crisis—is clearly no longer compatible with reality.[1]

1. Concerning Latin America, Brzezinski observed: "Latin American nationalism, more and more radical as it widens its popular base, will be directed with increasing animosity against the United States unless the United States rapidly shifts its own posture. Accordingly, it would be wise for the United States to make an explicit move to abandon the Monroe Doctrine and to concede that in the new global age geographic or

Only the "delayed development" of the Soviet Union, "an archaic religious community that experiences modernity existentially but not quite yet normatively," prevented wider realization of the fact that the end of ideology was already here. For the U.S., Brzezinski recommended "a great deal of patience," a more detached attitude toward world revolutionary processes, and a less anxious preoccupation with the Soviet Union. Instead of engaging in ancient diplomatic pastimes, we should make "a broader effort to contain the global tendencies toward chaos," while assisting the processes of change that will move the world toward the "community of developed nations."

The central concern of Brzezinski's book, as of the Carter administration's foreign policy, is with the modernization of the Third World. From the beginning, the administration has manifested a special, intense interest in the problems of the so-called Third World. But instead of viewing international developments in terms of the American national interest, as national interest is historically conceived, the architects of administration policy have viewed them in terms of a contemporary version of the same idea of progress that has traumatized Western imaginations since the Enlightenment.

In its current form, the concept of modernization involves more than industrialization, more than "political development" (whatever that is). It is used instead to designate ". . . the process through which a traditional or pre-technological society passes as it is transformed into a society characterized by machine technology, rational and secular attitudes, and highly differentiated social structures." Condorcet, Comte, Hegel, Marx, and Weber are all present in this view of history as the working out of the idea of modernity.

The crucial elements of the modernization concept have been clearly explicated by Samuel P. Huntington (who, despite a period at the National Security Council, was assuredly not the architect of the administration's policy). The modernization paradigm, Huntington has observed, postulates an ongoing process of change: complex, because it involves all dimensions of human life in society; systemic, because its elements interact in predictable, necessary ways; global, because all societies will, necessarily, pass through the transition from traditional to modern; lengthy, because time is required to modernize economic and social organization, character, and culture; phased, because each modernizing society must pass through essentially the

---

hemispheric contiguity no longer need be politically decisive. Nothing could be healthier for Pan-American relations than for the United States to place them on the same level as its relations with the rest of the world, confining itself to emphasis on cultural-political affinities (as it does with Western Europe) and economic-social obligations (as it does with less developed countries)."

same stages; homogenizing, because it tends toward the convergence and interdependence of societies; irreversible, because the direction of change is "given" in the relation of the elements of the process; progressive, in the sense that it is desirable, and in the long run provides significant benefits to the affiliated people.

Although the modernization paradigm has proved a sometimes useful as well as influential tool in social science, it has become the object of searching critiques that have challenged one after another of its central assumptions. Its shortcomings as an analytical tool pale, however, when compared to its inadequacies as a framework for thinking about foreign policy, where its principal effects are to encourage the view that events are manifestations of deep historical forces which cannot be controlled and that the best any government can do is to serve as a "midwife" to history, helping events to move where they are already headed.

This perspective on contemporary events is optimistic in the sense that it foresees continuing human progress; deterministic in the sense that it perceives events as fixed by processes over which persons and policies can have but little influence; moralistic in the sense that it perceives history and U.S. policy as having moral ends; cosmopolitan in the sense that it attempts to view the world not from the perspective of American interests or intentions but from the perspective of the modernizing nation and the "end" of history. It identifies modernization with both revolution and morality, and U.S. policy with all three.

The idea that it is "forces" rather than people which shape events recurs each time an administration spokesman articulates or explains policy. The President, for example, assured us in February of this year:

> The revolution in Iran is a product of deep social, political, religious, and economic factors growing out of the history of Iran itself.

And of Asia he said:

> At this moment there is turmoil or change in various countries from one end of the Indian Ocean to the other; some turmoil as in Indochina is the product of age-old enmities, inflamed by rivalries for influence by conflicting forces. Stability in some other countries is being shaken by the process of modernization, the search for national significance, or the desire to fulfill legitimate human hopes and human aspirations.

Harold Saunders, Assistant Secretary for Near Eastern and South

17

Asian Affairs, commenting on "instability" in Iran and the Horn of Africa, states:

> We, of course, recognize that fundamental changes are taking place across this area of western Asia and northeastern Africa—economic modernization, social change, a revival of religion, resurgent nationalism, demands for broader popular participation in the political process. These changes are generated by forces within each country.

Or here is Anthony Lake, chief of the State Department's Policy Planning staff, on South Africa:

> Change will come in South Africa. The welfare of the people there, and American interests, will be profoundly affected by the way in which it comes. The question is whether it will be peaceful or not.

Brzezinski makes the point still clearer. Speaking as chief of the National Security Council, he has assured us that the struggles for power in Asia and Africa are really only incidents along the route to modernization:

> ... all the developing countries in the arc from northeast Asia to southern Africa continue to search for viable forms of government capable of managing the process of modernization.

No matter that the invasions, coups, civil wars, and political struggles of less violent kinds that one sees all around do not *seem* to be incidents in a global personnel search for someone to manage the modernization process. Neither Brzezinski nor anyone else seems bothered by the fact that the political participants in that arc from northeast Asia to southern Africa do not *know* that they are "searching for viable forms of government capable of managing the process of modernization." The motives and intentions of real persons are no more relevant to the modernization paradigm than they are to the Marxist view of history. Viewed from this level of abstraction, it is the "forces" rather than the people that count.

So what if the "deep historical forces" at work in such diverse places as Iran, the Horn of Africa, Southeast Asia, Central America, and the United Nations look a lot like Russians or Cubans? Having moved past what the President calls our "inordinate fear of Communism," identified by him with the cold war, we should, we are told, now be capable of distinguishing Soviet and Cuban "machinations," which anyway exist mainly in the minds of cold warriors and others guilty of over-simplifying the world, from evolutionary changes, which seem to be the only kind that actually occur.

18

What can a U.S. President faced with such complicated, inexorable, impersonal processes *do*? The answer, offered again and again by the President and his top officials, is, not much. Since events are not caused by human decisions, they cannot be stopped or altered by them. Brzezinski, for example, has said, "We recognize that the world is changing under the influence of forces no government can control...." And Cyrus Vance has cautioned: "The fact is that we can no more stop change than Canute could still the waters."

The Carter administration's essentially deterministic and apolitical view of contemporary events discourages an active American response and encourages passivity. The American inability to influence events in Iran became the President's theme song:

> Those who argue that the U.S. should *or could* intervene directly to thwart [the revolution in Iran] are wrong about the realities of Iran.... We have encouraged *to the limited extent of our own ability* the public support for the Bakhtiar government.... How long [the Shah] will be out of Iran, we have no way to determine. Future events and his own desires will determine that.... It is impossible for anyone to anticipate all future political events.... Even if we had been able to anticipate events that were going to take place in Iran or in other countries, obviously our ability to determine those events is very limited [emphasis added].

Vance made the same point:

> In Iran our policy throughout the current crisis has been based on the fact that only Iranians can resolve the fundamental political issues which they now confront.

Where once upon a time an American President might have sent Marines to assure the protection of American strategic interests, there is no room for force in this world of progress and self-determination. Force, the President told us at Notre Dame, does not work; that is the lesson he extracted from Vietnam. It offers only "superficial" solutions. Concerning Iran, he said:

> Certainly we have no desire or ability to intrude massive forces into Iran or any other country to determine the outcome of domestic political issues. This is something that we have no intention of ever doing in another country. We've tried this once in Vietnam. It didn't work, as you well know.

There was nothing unique about Iran. In Nicaragua, the climate and language were different but the "historical forces" and the U.S.

response were the same. Military intervention was out of the question. Assistant Secretary of State Viron Vaky described as "unthinkable" the "use of U.S. military power to intervene in the internal affairs of another American republic." Vance provided parallel assurances for Africa, asserting that we would not try to match Cuban and Soviet activities there.

What *is* the function of foreign policy under these conditions? It is to understand the processes of change and then, like Marxists, to align ourselves with history, hoping to contribute a bit of stability along the way. And this, administration spokesmen assure us, is precisely what we are doing. The Carter administration has defined the U.S. national interest in the Third World as identical with the putative end of the modernization process. Vance put this with characteristic candor in a recent statement when he explained that U.S. policy vis-à-vis the Third World is "grounded in the conviction that we best serve our interest there by supporting the efforts of developing nations to advance their economic well-being and preserve their political independence." Our "commitment to the promotion of constructive change worldwide" (Brzezinski's words) has been vouchsafed in every conceivable context.

But there is a problem. The conceivable contexts turn out to be mainly those in which non-Communist autocracies are under pressure from revolutionary guerrillas. Since Moscow is the aggressive, expansionist power today, it is more often than not insurgents, encouraged and armed by the Soviet Union, who challenge the status quo. The American commitment to "change" in the abstract ends up by aligning us tacitly with Soviet clients and irresponsible extremists like the Ayatollah Khomeini or, in the end, Yasir Arafat.

So far, assisting "change" has not led the Carter administration to undertake the destabilization of a *Communist* country. The principles of self-determination and nonintervention are thus both selectively applied. We seem to accept the status quo in Communist nations (in the name of "diversity" and national autonomy), but not in nations ruled by "right-wing" dictators or white oligarchies. Concerning China, for example, Brzezinski has observed: "We recognize that the PRC and we have different ideologies and economic and political systems....We harbor neither the hope nor the desire that through extensive contacts with China we can remake that nation into the American image. Indeed, we accept our differences." Of Southeast Asia, the President noted in February:

> Our interest is to promote peace and the withdrawal of outside forces and not to become embroiled in the conflict

among Asian nations. And, in general, our interest is to promote the health and the development of individual societies, not to a pattern cut exactly like ours in the United States but tailored rather to the hopes and the needs and desires of the peoples involved.

But the administration's position shifts sharply when South Africa is discussed. For example, Anthony Lake asserted in late 1978:

> ...We have indicated to South Africa the fact that if it does not make significant progress toward racial equality, its relations with the international community, including the United States, are bound to deteriorate.
>
> Over the years, we have tried through a series of progressive steps to demonstrate that the U.S. cannot and will not be associated with the continued practice of apartheid.

As to Nicaragua, Hodding Carter III said in February 1979:

> The unwillingness of the Nicaraguan government to accept the [OAS] group's proposal, the resulting prospects for renewal and polarization, and the human-rights situation in Nicaragua...unavoidably affect the kind of relationships we can maintain with that government....

And Carter commented on Latin American autocracies:

> My government will not be deterred from protecting human rights, including economic and social rights, in whatever ways we can. We prefer to take actions that are positive, but where nations persist in serious violations of human rights, we will continue to demonstrate that there are costs to the flagrant disregard of international standards.

Something very odd is going on here. How does an administration that desires to let people work out their own destinies get involved in determined efforts at reform in South Africa, Zaire, Nicaragua, El Salvador, and elsewhere? How can an administration committed to nonintervention in Cambodia and Vietnam announce that it "will not be deterred" from righting wrongs in South Africa? What should be made of an administration that sees the U.S. interest as identical with economic modernization and political independence and yet heedlessly endangers the political independence of Taiwan, a country whose success in economic modernization and egalitarian distribution of wealth is unequaled in Asia? The contrast is as striking as that between the administration's frenzied speed in recognizing the new dictatorship in Nicaragua and its continuing refusal to recognize the elected government of Zimbabwe Rhodesia, or its refusal to maintain any presence in Zimbabwe Rhodesia while staffing a U.S. Information Office in Cuba. Not only are there ideology and a double standard at work here, the ideology neither fits nor explains reality, and the double standard involves the administration in the wholesale contradiction of its own principles.

Inconsistencies are a familiar part of politics in most societies. Usually, however, governments behave hypocritically when their principles conflict with the national interest. What makes the inconsistencies of the Carter administration noteworthy are, first, the administration's moralism—which renders it especially vulnerable to charges of hypocrisy; and, second, the administration's predilection for policies that violate the strategic and economic interests of the United States. The administration's conception of national interest borders on doublethink: it finds friendly powers to be guilty representatives of the status quo and views the triumph of unfriendly groups as beneficial to America's "true interests."

This logic is quite obviously reinforced by the prejudices and preferences of many administration officials. Traditional autocracies are, in general and in their very nature, deeply offensive to modern American sensibilities. The notion that public affairs should be ordered on the basis of kinship, friendship, and other personal relations rather than on the basis of "rational" standards violates our conception of justice and efficiency. The preference for stability rather than change is also disturbing to Americans whose whole national experience rests on the principles of change, growth, and progress. The extremes of wealth and poverty characteristic of traditional societies also offend us, the more so since the poor are usually *very* poor and bound to their squalor by a hereditary allocation of role. Moreover, the relative lack of concern of rich, comfortable rulers for the poverty, ignorance, and disease of "their" people is likely to be interpreted by Americans as moral dereliction pure and simple. The truth is that Americans can hardly bear such societies and such rulers. Confronted with them, our vaunted cultural relativism evaporates and we become as censorious as Cotton Mather confronting sin in New England.

But if the politics of traditional and semi-traditional autocracy is nearly antithetical to our own—at both the symbolic and the operational level—the rhetoric of progressive revolutionaries sounds much better to us; their symbols are much more acceptable. One reason that some modern Americans prefer "socialist" to traditional autocracies is that the former have embraced modernity and have adopted modern modes and perspectives, including an instrumental, manipulative, functional orientation toward most social, cultural, and personal affairs; a profession of universalistic norms; an emphasis on reason, science, education, and progress; a de-emphasis of the sacred; and "rational," bureaucratic organizations. They speak our language.

Because socialism of the Soviet/Chinese/Cuban variety is an ideology rooted in a version of the same values that sparked the Enlightenment and the democratic revolutions of the 18th century; because it is modern and not traditional; because it postulates goals that appeal to Christian as well as to secular values (brotherhood of man, elimination of power as a mode of human relations), it is highly congenial to many Americans at the symbolic level. Marxist revolutionaries speak the language of a hopeful future while traditional autocrats speak the language of an unattractive past. Because left-wing revolutionaries invoke the symbols and values of democracy—emphasizing egalitarianism rather than hierarchy and privilege, liberty rather than order, activity rather than passivity—they are again and again accepted as partisans in the cause of freedom and democracy.

Nowhere is the affinity of liberalism, Christianity, and Marxist socialism more apparent than among liberals who are "duped" time after time into supporting "liberators" who turn out to be totalitarians, and among Left-leaning clerics whose attraction to a secular style of "redemptive community" is stronger than their outrage at the hostility of socialist regimes to religion. In Jimmy Carter—egalitarian, optimist, liberal, Christian—the tendency to be repelled by frankly nondemocratic rulers and hierarchical societies is almost as strong as the tendency to be attracted to the idea of popular revolution, liberation, and progress. Carter is, *par excellence*, the kind of liberal most likely to confound revolution with idealism, change with progress, optimism with virtue.

Where concern about "socialist encirclement," Soviet expansion, and traditional conceptions of the national interest inoculated his predecessors against such easy equations, Carter's doctrine of national interest and modernization encourages support for all change that takes place in the name of "the people," regardless of its "superficial" Marxist or anti-American content. Any lingering doubt about whether the U.S. should, in case of conflict, support a "tested friend" such as the Shah, or a friendly power such as Zimbabwe Rhodesia against an opponent who despises us is resolved by reference to our "true," our "long-range" interests.

Stephen Rosenfeld of the Washington *Post* described the commitment of the Carter administration to this sort of "progressive liberalism":

> The Carter administration came to power, after all, committed precisely to reducing the centrality of strategic competition with Moscow in American foreign policy, and to extending the United States' association with what it was prepared to accept as legitimate wave-of-the-future popular movements around the world—first of all with the victorious movement in Vietnam.
>
> . . . Indochina was supposed to be the state on which Americans could demonstrate their "post-Vietnam" intent to come to terms with the progressive popular element that Kissinger, the villain, had denied.

In other words, the Carter administration, Rosenfeld tells us, came to power resolved not to assess international developments in the light of "cold-war" perspectives but to accept at face value the claim of revolutionary groups to represent "popular" aspirations and "progressive" forces—regardless of the ties of these revolutionaries to the Soviet Union. To this end, overtures were made looking to the "normalization" of relations with Vietnam, Cuba, and the Chinese People's Republic, and steps were taken to cool relations with South Korea, South Africa, Nicaragua, the Philippines, and others. These moves followed naturally from the conviction that the U.S. had, as our enemies said, been on the wrong side of history in supporting the status quo and opposing revolution.

One might have thought that this perspective would have been undermined by events in Southeast Asia since the triumph of "progressive" forces there over the "agents of reaction." To cite Rosenfeld again:

> In this administration's time, Vietnam has been transformed for much of American public opinion, from a country wronged by the U.S. to one revealing a brutal essence of its own.
>
> This has been a quiet but major trauma to the Carter people (as to all liberals) scarring their self-confidence and their claim on public trust alike.

Presumably, however, the barbarity of the "progressive" governments in Cambodia and Vietnam has been less traumatic for the President and his chief advisers than for Rosenfeld, since there is little evidence of changed predispositions at crucial levels of the White House and the State Department. The President continues to behave as before—not like a man who abhors autocrats but like one who abhors only right-wing autocrats.

In fact, high officials in the Carter administration understand better than they seem to the aggressive, expansionist character of contemporary Soviet behavior in Africa, the Middle East, Southeast Asia, the Indian Ocean, Central America, and the Caribbean. But although the Soviet/Cuban role in Grenada, Nicaragua, and El Salvador (plus the transfer of MIG-23's to Cuba) had already prompted resumption of surveillance of Cuba (which in turn confirmed the presence of a Soviet combat brigade), the President's eagerness not to "heat up" the climate of public opinion remains stronger than his commitment to speak the truth to the American people. His statement on Nicaragua clearly reflects these priorities:

> It's a mistake for Americans to assume or to claim that every time an evolutionary change takes place in this hemisphere that somehow it's a result of secret, massive Cuban intervention. The fact in Nicaragua is that the Somoza regime lost the confidence of the people. To bring about an orderly transition there, our effort was to let the people of Nicaragua ultimately make the decision on who would be their leader— what form of government they should have.

This statement, which presumably represents the President's best thinking on the matter, is illuminating. Carter's effort to dismiss concern about military events in this specific country as a manifestation of a national proclivity for seeing "Cuban machinations" under every bed constitutes a shocking effort to falsify reality. There was no question in Nicaragua of "evolutionary change" or of attributing such change to Castro's agents. There was only a question about the appropriate U.S. response to a military struggle in a country whose location gives it strategic importance out of proportion to its size or strength.

But that is not all. The rest of the President's statement graphically illustrates the blinding power of ideology on his interpretation of events. When he says that "the Somoza regime lost the confidence of the people," the President implies that the regime had previously rested on the confidence of "the people," but that the situation had now changed. In fact, the Somoza regime had never rested on popular will (but instead on manipulation, force, and habit), and was not being ousted by it. It was instead succumbing to arms and soldiers. However, the assumption that the armed conflict of Sandinistas and Somozistas was the military equivalent of a national referendum enabled the President to imagine that it could be, and should be, settled by the people of Nicaragua. For this pious sentiment even to seem true the President would have had to be unaware that insurgents were receiving a great many arms from other non-Nicaraguans; and that the U.S had played a significant role in disarming the Somoza regime.

The President's mistakes and distortions are all fashionable ones.

25

His assumptions are those of people who want badly to be on the progressive side in conflicts between "rightist" autocracy and "leftist" challenges, and to prefer the latter, almost regardless of the probable consequences.

To be sure, neither the President, nor Vance, nor Brzezinski *desires* the proliferation of Soviet-supported regimes. Each has asserted his disapproval of Soviet "interference" in the modernization process. But each, nevertheless, remains willing to "destabilize" friendly or neutral autocracies without any assurance that they will not be replaced by reactionary totalitarian theocracies, totalitarian Soviet client states, or worst of all, by murderous fanatics of the Pol Pot variety.

The foreign policy of the Carter administration fails not for lack of good intentions but for lack of realism about the nature of traditional versus revolutionary autocracies and the relation of each to the American national interest. Only intellectual fashion and the tyranny of Right/Left thinking prevent intelligent men of good will from perceiving the *facts* that traditional authoritarian governments are less repressive than revolutionary autocracies, that they are more susceptible of liberalization, and that they are more compatible with U.S interests. The evidence on all these points is clear enough.

Surely it is now beyond reasonable doubt that the present governments of Vietnam, Cambodia, Laos are much more repressive than those of the despised previous rulers; that the government of the People's Republic of China is more repressive than that of Taiwan, that North Korea is more repressive than South Korea, and so forth. This is the most important lesson of Vietnam and Cambodia. It is not new but it is a gruesome reminder of harsh facts.

From time to time a truly bestial ruler can come to power in either type of autocracy—Idi Amin, Papa Doc Duvalier, Joseph Stalin, Pol Pot are examples—but neither type regularly produces such moral monsters (though democracy regularly prevents their accession to power). There are, however, *systemic* differences between traditional and revolutionary autocracies that have a predictable effect on their degree of repressiveness. Generally speaking, traditional autocrats tolerate social inequities, brutality, and poverty while revolutionary autocracies create them.

Traditional autocrats leave in place existing allocations of wealth, power, status, and other resources which in most traditional societies favor an affluent few and maintain masses in poverty. But they worship traditional gods and observe traditional taboos. They do not disturb the habitual rhythms of work and leisure, habitual places of residence, habitual patterns of family and personal relations. Because

26

the miseries of traditional life are familiar, they are bearable to ordinary people who, growing up in the society, learn to cope, as children born to untouchables in India acquire the skills and attitudes necessary for survival in the miserable roles they are destined to fill. Such societies create no refugees.

Precisely the opposite is true of revolutionary Communist regimes. They create refugees by the million because they claim jurisdiction over the whole life of the society and make demands for change that so violate internalized values and habits that inhabitants flee by the tens of thousands in the remarkable expectation that their attitudes, values, and goals will "fit" better in a foreign country than in their native land.

The former deputy chairman of Vietnam's National Assembly from 1976 to his defection early in August 1979, Hoang Van Hoan, described recently the impact of Vietnam's ongoing revolution on that country's more than one million Chinese inhabitants:

> They have been expelled from places they have lived in for generations. They have been dispossessed of virtually all possessions—their lands, their houses. They have been driven into areas called new economic zones, but they have not been given any aid.
>
> How can they eke out a living in such conditions reclaiming new land? They gradually die for a number of reasons—diseases, the hard life. They also die of humiliation.

It is not only the Chinese who have suffered in Southeast Asia since the "liberation," and it is not only in Vietnam that the Chinese suffer. By the end of 1978 more than six million refugees had fled countries ruled by Marxist governments. In spite of walls, fences, guns, and sharks, the steady stream of people fleeing revolutionary utopias continues.

There is a damning contrast between the number of refugees created by Marxist regimes and those created by other autocracies: more than a million Cubans have left their homeland since Castro's rise (one refugee for every nine inhabitants) as compared to about 35,000 each from Argentina, Brazil, and Chile. In Africa more than five times as many refugees have fled Guinea and Guinea Bissau as have left Zimbabwe Rhodesia, suggesting that civil war and racial discrimination are easier for most people to bear than Marxist-style liberation.

Moreover, the history of this century provides no grounds for expecting that radical totalitarian regimes will transform themselves. At the moment there is a far greater likelihood of progressive liberalization and democratization in the governments of Brazil, Argentina, and Chile than in the government of Cuba; in Taiwan than in the

People's Republic of China; in South Korea than in North Korea; in Zaire than in Angola; and so forth.

Since many traditional autocracies permit limited contestation and participation, it is not impossible that U.S. policy could effectively encourage this process of liberalization and democratization, provided that the effort is not made at a time when the incumbent government is fighting for its life against violent adversaries, and that proposed reforms are aimed at producing gradual change rather than perfect democracy overnight. To accomplish this, policy-makers are needed who understand how actual democracies have actually come into being. History is a better guide than good intentions.

A realistic policy which aims at protecting our own interest and assisting the capacities for self-determination of less developed nations will need to face the unpleasant fact that, if victorious, violent insurgency headed by Marxist revolutionaries is unlikely to lead to anything but totalitarian tyranny. Armed intellectuals citing Marx and supported by Soviet-bloc arms and advisers will almost surely not turn out to be agrarian reformers, or simple nationalists, or democratic socialists. However incomprehensible it may be to some, Marxist revolutionaries are not contemporary embodiments of the Americans who wrote the Declaration of Independence, and they will not be content with establishing a broad-based coalition in which they have only one voice among many.

It may not always be easy to distinguish between democratic and totalitarian agents of change, but it is also not too difficult. Authentic democratic revolutionaries aim at securing governments based on the consent of the governed and believe that ordinary men are capable of using freedom, knowing their own interest, choosing rulers. They do not, like the current leaders in Nicaragua, assume that it will be necessary to postpone elections for three to five years during which time they can "cure" the false consciousness of almost everyone.

If, moreover, revolutionary leaders describe the United States as the scourge of the 20th century, the enemy of freedom-loving people, the perpetrator of imperialism, racism, colonialism, genocide, war, then they are not authentic democrats or, to put it mildly, friends. Groups which define themselves as enemies should be treated as enemies. The United States is not in fact a racist, colonial power, it does not practice genocide, it does not threaten world peace with expansionist activities. In the last decade especially we have practiced remarkable forbearance everywhere and undertaken the "unilateral restraints on defense spending" recommend by Brzezinski as appropriate for the technetronic era. We have also moved further, faster, in eliminating domestic racism than any multiracial society in the world or in history.

For these reasons and more, a posture of continuous self-abasement and apology vis-à-vis the Third World is neither morally necessary nor politically appropriate. No more is it necessary or appropriate to support vocal enemies of the United States because they invoke the rhetoric of popular liberation. It is not even necessary or appropriate for our leaders to forswear unilaterally the use of military force to counter military force. Liberal idealism need not be identical with masochism, and need not be incompatible with the defense of freedom and the national interest.

Democracy and Human Rights in Latin America: Toward a New Conceptualization

HOWARD J. WIARDA

The number of books and articles on Latin America's "struggle for democracy" runs into the legions. In much current foreign policy discussion, moreover, the issues of human rights and U.S. relations with authoritarian regimes have received a great deal of attention.[1] This paper deals with those issues (with special reference to the Iberic–Latin American context) and raises some troubling questions: Are democracy and human rights everywhere the same and universal?

NOTE: This article is based on a paper presented at the U.S. Department of State, Bureau of Inter-American Affairs, on January 25, 1977. An earlier version was presented at Lafayette College. The author thanks those at Lafayette and the Department of State who offered comments and raised questions, and acknowledges the suggestions of Keith Rosenn and Iêda Siqueira Wiarda which led to improvements in the written draft. The views expressed, however, are entirely those of the author and do not in any sense represent an official position.

1. Amnesty International has issued numerous reports on human rights violations in Latin America; the New York Times has published many accounts; the U.S. Department of State has submitted to the House International Relations Committee detailed reports on human rights conditions abroad; congressional hearings have been held; the report of the Commission on United States–Latin American Relations (the "Linowitz Commission") urged a stronger emphasis on human rights; and, of course, President Carter and his key advisers have referred repeatedly to human rights protection as a cornerstone of U.S. foreign policy. But see also, Marshall D. Shulman, "On Learning to Live with Authoritarian Regimes," Foreign Affairs, January 1977, pp. 325–338, and William P. Bundy, "Dictatorships and American Foreign Policy," Foreign Affairs, October 1975, pp. 51–60.

Are they relevant in the same sense to all societies and in all time frames? And do grounds exist for the hope of exporting democracy and human rights to other lands and culture-areas?

The difficulty is that terms such as "democracy," "human rights," "representative rule," "pluralism," "freedom," "participation" and "social justice" mean different things, convey different connotations or enjoy differential legitimacy from society to society. Moreover, even in a single society (obviously including the United States), these concepts may change over time, relating generally to broad cultural, socioeconomic and political transformations. We have long been aware of such differences of meaning with regard to the "peoples' democracies," but it is here suggested that even within the "West" the above concepts and terms of reference may carry, among different societies, quite distinct meanings and understandings. Neither adequate grounds for moral judgment, nor the basis for enlightened and rational foreign policy can be established until these differences are clearly understood. Although the focus here is on Iberia and Latin America, on what democracy and human rights mean in that culture-area, the following discussion also has relevance to Africa, Asia and perhaps elsewhere.

In offering such a broad view, one must sometimes gloss over the nuances, national variations and ambiguities that exist, elements which must be taken into consideration in any final and definitive analysis of the subject. Obviously, the situation of democracy and human rights in present-day Colombia, Costa Rica and Venezuela is different from that in Argentina, Chile and Paraguay. Although we must certainly be cognizant of these variations, differentiate carefully among the diverse nations of the area, and note how they change over time, the emphasis here will be on the common and continuous features. My purpose is to offer a way of thinking about the meaning and practice of democracy and human rights in Iberia and Latin America, as distinguished from the North American conception, and to present an ideal-typical construct which stresses the similarities in the Iberic–Latin American political culture as compared with that of the United States. Sound policy, of course, demands that each country be examined on an individual basis, but before that can be done, an understanding must be achieved of the common context in which such individual variations take place. The present article is conceived, therefore, not as a set of concrete prescriptions to be applied in individual cases but, perhaps more fundamentally, as an essential prelude before any such policy measures can be intelligently thought about.

Democracy and Human Rights:
Applying a North American Perspective

In 1945, the Inter-American Conference on the Problems of War and Peace, meeting at Chapultepec, Mexico, adopted a resolution calling for the international protection of human rights. At the Bogotá Conference in 1948, the Latin American nations adopted the Charter of the Organization of American States and the American Declaration of the Rights and Duties of Man, the latter document based largely on the UN Declaration of Human Rights, to which the Latin American States are also signatories. In their own constitutions, too, the Latin American nations have consistently embraced the principles of republican government, separation of powers and human rights.[2] Because of such documents, we often assume that Latin America uses such terms in the same way as the United States.

A useful starting point for the discussion of just how "democratic" Latin America is, and how its interpretation of "human rights" may differ from that of North America, is the influential, periodic survey of "democracy" and its "progress" in Latin America by Russell H. Fitzgibbon and his collaborators.[3] The following criteria, among others, are included in their definition and measures:

1. the degree to which freedom of the press, speech and assembly exist;
2. whether there are free elections and honestly counted votes;
3. whether freedom exists for political party organization, for party opposition in the congress, for opposition groups generally;
4. whether there is an independent, coequal judiciary and congress;

2. See Kenneth L. Karst and Keith S. Rosenn, *Law and Development in Latin America* (Berkeley: University of California Press, 1975).

3. Fitzgibbon, "Measurement of Latin American Political Phenomena: A Statistical Experiment," *American Political Science Review*, June 1951, pp. 517-523; Fitzgibbon, "A Statistical Evaluation of Latin American Democracy," *Western Political Quarterly*, September 1956, pp. 607-619; Fitzgibbon and Kenneth F. Johnson, "Measurement of Latin American Political Change," *American Political Science Review*, September 1961, pp. 515-526; Fitzgibbon, "Measuring Democratic Change in Latin America," *Journal of Politics*, February 1967, pp. 129-166; Johnson, "Measuring the Scholarly Image of Latin American Democracy, 1945-70," in *Statistical Abstract of Latin America* (Los Angeles: UCLA Latin American Center, 1976); Johnson, "Scholarly Images of Latin American Political Democracy in 1975," *Latin American Research Review*, Summer 1976, pp. 127-138; and Johnson, "Research Perspectives on the Revised Fitzgibbon-Johnson Index of the Image of Political Democracy in Latin America, 1945-75," in James W. Wilkie and Kenneth Ruddle, eds., *Quantitative Latin American Studies* (Los Angeles: UCLA Latin American Center, 1977), pp. 87-91.

In the more recent formulations, Professor Johnson distinguishes usefully between Latin American democracy per se and the various nations' reputations for democracy as perceived by the U.S. scholars surveyed. He has also introduced a number of other qualifications in order to remove some of the ethnocentrism from the original index.

5. the degree of accountability for the collection and expenditure of public funds;
6. whether there is civilian supremacy over the military;
7. whether political life is free from ecclesiastical controls;
8. the strength of independent local government; and
9. whether there is representative, participatory and pluralist democratic government.

Few of us would disagree with these values and institutions. But it may be argued that this is so because the concepts and criteria used correspond closely to the liberal, Lockean, Anglo-American tradition and polity. The Fitzgibbon definition, to which most of us in the United States subscribe, has in it a powerful Montesquieuian, Jeffersonian, Madisonian bias. It is based on contract theory and the civil law tradition. It stems directly from the United States Constitution and the Bill of Rights. Its model is the independent yeoman and individualist of the New England ideal, grassroots democracy and popular (electoral) participation, separation of powers and of the military and ecclesiastical realms from the political, and a pluralistic and egalitarian polity with a hallowed tradition of respect for individual human rights. The question is whether these fundamental characteristics apply equally and in the same sense to Iberia and Latin America, or whether they represent instead a peculiarly North American set of expectations and practices inapplicable in culture-areas other than our own.

A second difficulty with the Fitzgibbon formulation, besides its ethnocentrism, is that it ignores those features in the Latin American constitutions, features at least as prominent as the liberal-democratic ones, that enshrine authoritarian rule, corporate privilege and constitutional and legal restrictions on human rights. Reserving further discussion for later, let us for now emphasize that authoritarian rule in Latin America does not necessarily mean a usurpation of the laws and constitution but often represents a new emphasis on those features that the Fitzgibbon criteria ignore.[4]

Third, there is no sense in the Fitzgibbon studies that "freedom of the press," "elections," "opposition," etc. may mean something different in Luso-Hispanic civilization and law than they do in the Anglo-American, or that they may exist at different levels of popular acceptance and legitimacy. Keeping in mind the vicissitudes within nations as well as the variations among them, let us examine the Fitzgibbon criteria one at a time, as a way of examining both what

4. See the comment of Dale Furnish ("Military governments . . . are an accepted part of the legal system"; they also govern "through laws and acts constrained by custom and constitutional privileges") in "The Hierarchy of Peruvian Laws: Context for Law and Development," *American Journal of Comparative Law*, Winter 1971, pp. 91-120.

Iberia and Latin America generally understand by these terms and how these understandings are distinct from those of North America.

1. Freedom of the Press, Speech, Assembly. The freedoms of press, speech and assembly are a part of the Latin American legal and constitutional tradition, and some countries, to a greater or lesser degree, have striven to uphold them. But, even allowing for the formal presence of such freedoms in Iberia and Latin America and for their implementation in some countries in ways that parallel U.S. practice, it is clear that the meaning of these terms in the Iberic–Latin American culture-area reflects different understandings and expectations than in the North American area. These liberties do not enjoy the hallowed place they do in the U.S. Bill of Rights, nor are they enshrined as inviolable principles. To a far greater degree than in the United States, freedom in Iberia and Latin America also implies obligations and duties, including the obligation to obey those in authority. Liberty carries with it the obligation for self-censorship and the exercise of prior restraint.

The lists of human and social rights contained in the Latin American constitutions, or in their injunctions to democracy and representative rule, constitute ideals, aspirations and future goals for society to achieve. They are not presumed to correspond to actual operating reality, nor is any regime expected to live up to them completely. Frequently, human rights (*derechos*) must be subordinated to (a) even more fundamental corporate group rights (*fueros*), (b) the notion of the "common good" (generally, as defined by the state), and (c) the even higher-order requirements of natural, eternal or, if one wishes, divine law (although even in Catholic Latin America the latter is seldom explicitly invoked). There is, in short, a hierarchy of laws which command varying obedience: what in the United States is considered a fundamental right often occupies a third- or fourth-order priority in Latin America. Human rights are respected and honored, but they may be subordinated to such perceived higher-order priorities as the unity and integrity of the state. When the two conflict, it is most frequently individual human rights that give way.[5]

Moreover, there are provisions contained in the Iberian and Latin American constitutions (e.g., "emergency" clauses and those providing for the declaration of a "state of siege") that make it possible to suspend human rights altogether, sometimes indefinitely. Freedom of

5. The best brief discussion is John Henry Merryman, *The Civil Law Tradition: An Introduction to the Legal Systems of Western Europe and Latin America* (Stanford, Calif.: Stanford University Press, 1969). Also see the special issue of the *American Journal of Comparative Law* (Winter 1971) dealing with "Law and Development in Latin America."

the press or of assembly may legitimately be curbed if the peace and order of the nation are threatened. Of course, there are abuses of these clauses, but the point is that historically the rights contained in the U.S. Constitution have in Latin America seldom been considered inalienable. Rather, it is the state itself that is the arbiter and dispenser of rights and justice, and what the state gives, it can also revoke. Even in those habeas corpus, writ of personal security, and *amparo* cases where an individual or group challenges the suspension of human rights, it is the state, acting in the name of some higher-order common good, that must ultimately decide.[6]

2. Elections. Electoral politics and elections have also become both important and imbedded in Latin American law and constitution. In Colombia, Costa Rica and Venezuela, and in some other countries at other times, competitive elections have become a regular part of the political process. But in most Latin American countries, even in some of those mentioned, elections do not necessarily convey definitive legitimacy to a regime or an individual for a prescribed term. Alternative routes to power, such as the skillfully executed coup d'état or the heroic guerrilla struggle, remain open and also carry potential for gaining legitimacy.[7] Furthermore, even when electoral results are accepted in principle, numerous legal and constitutional means exist to nullify their impact. The Brazilian election in 1960 of João Goulart, who was allowed to assume the presidency—temporarily, as it turned out—only after agreeing to transfer most of his authority to the congress, provides a dramatic case in point.

Additionally, when elections do occur and do count, seldom is there a genuine choice; rather, the Bonapartist or Gaullist model tends to be followed. Elections often take a plebiscitary form, being used more to ratify a government-in-power than to provide real choice. Moreover, party pacts and accords are employed to provide for continuity (and monopoly) and to exclude other challengers. Of course, genuinely competitive elections do occur, but even in those countries often thought of as democratic (Colombia, Venezuela, Costa Rica, perhaps Mexico and the Dominican Republic), one is struck by the tendency toward oligopoly and accord within and among the major parties and, hence, the shutting off of possible alternatives. Thus, two potentially conflicting functions can be served at once: the opposition and the ruling groups can have the "democratic" electoral campaign

6. Karst and Rosenn, pt. 2, esp. pp. 232ff.

7. Charles W. Anderson, *Politics and Economic Change in Latin America* (Princeton, N.J.: Van Nostrand, 1967), chap. 4.

both can agree is necessary, and the government "party" can generally "have" its election.[8]

3. Party Freedom and Loyal Opposition. Freedom for opposition groups and parties is generally allowed in principle in Latin America, but this freedom, too, is often constrained and subject to higher priorities. The constraints derive both from the legal-constitutional framework and the overall political culture.

The law and constitution provide the executive with ample power to limit opposition party activity or to suspend opposition functions altogether. The more liberal and democractic regimes of Latin America have seldom been inclined to use the full gamut of the powers at their disposal, but the power is there nonetheless. Also, there is often rather little "party politics" in the Anglo-American sense. One can easily overdraw the differences, but they remain important. In the U.S. system, parties are usually viewed as at the center of politics, carrying out many important functions and providing just about the only legitimate route to power. Throughout Latin America, in contrast, and again with several notable exceptions, parties operate at the margin of the public law, frequently enjoying neither respect nor much legitimacy. The hurly-burly and chaos of party competition is frequently viewed as intolerable: divisive party politics is seen as detracting from the unity and coherence of the state. Hence, a "technocratic" regime devoid of "politics" and parties is usually much preferred.

Under the organicist, monistic conceptions that so pervade Iberia and Latin America, moreover, opposition is almost by definition subversive, traitorous and something to be dealt with harshly. A "loyal opposition," then, is almost a contradiction in terms. Finally, even where parties are organized, the party label is often avoided. One forms a "movement" or a "civic-action association," but seldom a party. Political parties tend to become official appendages of the regime, bureaucratic state machines, national patronage agencies, or personalist vehicles. Rarely do they maintain an independent existence. Terms like "party freedom" or "opposition freedom" must be understood in this light.[9]

4. Independent, Coequal Congress and Judiciary. Checks and balances à la Montesquieu exist in the formal laws and constitutions of

8. For one such case, see Steven Ussach, "The Portuguese Presidential Election of 1958" (University of Massachusetts, Amherst, Department of Political Science, 1974).

9. Douglas Chalmers, "Parties and Society in Latin America," *Studies in Comparative International Development*, Summer 1972, pp. 102-130; Robert Dix, "Latin America: Opposition and Development," in Robert A. Dahl, ed., *Regimes and Opposition* (New Haven, Conn.: Yale University Press, 1973).

Latin America. But in those same laws and constitutions, as well as in hallowed tradition, centralized and unitary control is also enshrined. The extensive power of the executive, in the "Caesarist" or "imperial" traditions, and the weakness and lack of independence of the courts and legislatures, are familiar features of Latin America's political culture. Though lip service is often paid to "separation of powers," and though in some countries the legislature has gained prominence, the prevailing pattern has been presidential dominance.[10]

The strong executive is neither a quirk, aberration nor a sign of Latin American "underdevelopment." It is a logical outgrowth of the assumptions on which the polity is based. For under the prevailing organicist conception, government is "natural" and "good"—not "unnatural" or "bad," and therefore to be distrusted, as in the historical U.S. conception. If government is natural and good, there is little need to limit or check-and-balance it. One should not, therefore, look for a coequal congress or judiciary in a system where such has not been the tradition, in law, constitution or history.[11]

5. Public Funds and Accountability. Quite a sharp distinction is made in the United States between the public and the private weals. Abuses occur, but the fact that we are incensed when a congressman or vice-president enriches himself in public office illustrates the strict separation we seek to maintain. Our model of the good public servant is that of the Burkean savant idealized in our public-school civics courses: someone who is fair, responsible, serves the public interest, and strictly segregates private and public affairs.

In the Iberic–Latin American patrimonialist tradition, no such sharp division exists: the line between public and private is blurred. Historically, both private and public wealth were considered part of the ruler's domain. Land, water, mines and trading contracts could be granted in trust to individuals for development, but the crown always expected to receive a share of the profits and reserved the right to reclaim the grants it had made. Moreover, land grants and charters, virtually any service, involved mutual obligations and generally the payment of a fee. For any official document to be expedited required a favor, often monetary, in return. This is not to imply that North Americans are by nature honest and Latin Americans not. It is to say that "honesty" may mean different things in different contexts, that in

10. Glen Dealy, "The Tradition of Monistic Democracy in Latin America," in Howard J. Wiarda, ed., *Politics and Social Change in Latin America* (Amherst: University of Massachusetts Press, 1974), pp. 71-104; James Busey, "Observations on Latin American Constitutionalism," *The Americas*, July 1967, pp. 46-66.

11. Guenter Lewy, *Constitutionalism and Statecraft During the Golden Age of Spain* (Geneva: Droz, 1960).

the patrimonialist conception prevalent in Latin America, no strict separation between private and public weals is possible. Anyone who purports to measure accountability for the collection and expenditure of public funds must take these differences into account.[12]

6. Civilian Supremacy over the Military. Civilian supremacy is a major premise of the Anglo-American polities, but in Latin America, it is often circumscribed or nonexistent. One must not, of course, overstate the differences, for military influence in the United States has probably long been stronger than we usually presume, and in Latin America there are usually constitutional injunctions against the military exercising political functions. Yet in Latin America, no strict separation exists between the military and civilian spheres. When North Americans refer to "civil-military relations," a separation is implied that in Latin America does not always exist. The military is often the strongest "party," a fact recognized both by civilians and military men; and the result is that most political conflicts take the form not of a civilian-versus-military struggle, but of competing factions that overlap and crosscut the civilian and military spheres.

In addition, the military in Latin America is no mere interest group, in the U.S. sense, but an integral part of the bureaucratic system and inseparable from it. Stemming perhaps from the role of the military orders in the formation of the Spanish nation, the army is one of the fundamental props of the state system, with special responsibilities, prerogatives and functions. Even in the more democratic Latin American countries, the military has consistently acted at or close to the surface of power. The military, moreover, by law and constitution, has certain "higher-level" priorities to preserve order and tranquillity, maintain domestic peace, and exercise a "moderating" role in national affairs. The military serves almost literally as a fourth branch of government, having a duty to step into politics under certain circumstances. That the military stepped into power in Argentina, Chile and Uruguay should not be very surprising. What is shocking and repugnant, especially in Chile, is what the military did after it came to power.[13]

12. Patrimonialism is discussed in Reinhard Bendix, *Max Weber: An Intellectual Portrait* (New York: Doubleday, 1962), pp. 334-360. Also see Sidney M. Greenfield, *The Patrimonial State and Patron-Client Relations in Iberia and Latin America* (Amherst: University of Massachusetts, Program in Latin American Studies, Occasional Paper no. 1, 1976).

13. On the military's place and role, see Lawrence Graham, *Portugal: The Decline and Collapse of an Authoritarian Order* (Beverly Hills: Sage, 1971); Alfred Stepan, *The Military in Politics: Changing Patterns in Brazil* (Princeton, N.J.: Princeton University Press, 1971); and Robert A. Potash, *The Impact of Professionalism on the Twentieth Century Argentine Military* (Amherst: University of Massachusetts, Program in Latin American Studies, Occasional Paper no. 3, 1977).

7. Freedom from Ecclesiastic Controls. Much of what has been said of the military also applies to the Church. The Church is intimately a part of Iberian and Latin American culture, in terms of (a) the philosophic base of the political order and (b) the frequent fusion and mutual reinforcement of Catholicism and the legal, educational and social systems. As is the army, the Church is often a part of the state system and inseparable from it, having special obligations in the administration of schools, orphanages, hospitals and the defense of public morality and order. The Church is not a mere interest group but bears certain primary responsibilities in the political realm. Despite the sometimes formal separation of church and state in the Latin American constitutions, the reality is more ambiguous. The principle of "freedom of political life from ecclesiastic controls" is either meaningless or in need of further refinement.[14]

8. Strong, Independent Local Government. The principle of strong, independent local government also derives from the Anglo-American tradition, particularly the oft-romanticized New England town meeting. It is not an appropriate measure of Latin American democracy for several reasons. Despite difficulties of implementation, the Latin American pattern has been one of centralized, administrative rule from the top, rather than grassroots participatory democracy. As in most nations whose administration is based on the Napoleonic Code, little power has ever devolved upon the local units; instead, most local officials are appointed, and power is concentrated in the central state. There is little expectation at either the local or the national level that local government can or should be effective. The national regime usually must respect local charters, where they exist, and has some obligation to listen to local demands; but virtually all decisions are made in the capital city, and programs are implemented by the national government through its local agents. Local governments themselves have no power to tax or to devise educational or any other important local programs. Nor is there much expectation that they should.[15]

9. Representative, Participatory and Pluralist Government. Again, few of us would argue with the principle of representative, participatory and pluralist government. The difficulty is that what Iberic–Latin American civilization means by these terms frequently varies from the Anglo-American view.

14. Fredrick B. Pike, *The Conflict Between Church and State in Latin America* (New York: Knopf, 1964); Henry A. Landsberger, ed., *The Church and Social Change in Latin America* (Notre Dame, Ind.: University of Notre Dame Press, 1970).

15. Lawrence Graham, "Latin America: Illusion or Reality?" in Wiarda, ed.

"Representation" in Iberia and Latin America means not just geographic representation and "one man, one vote" but often implies representation of society's major functional or corporate groups. Although lip service (and sometimes more than that) is paid to the principle of equal representation, special groups and corporate elites frequently receive preferential treatment. The mere fact of birth does not carry with it the right to representation; rather, representation is earned through a "civilizing" process which usually includes incorporation of the individual into one of society's recognized component groups. Hence the frequent importance of (a) functionally representative legislatures and councils of state, (b) special access for those groups with "juridical personality," and (c) the mixture of corporate and individualistic modes of representation.[16]

"Participation" also takes place, generally through officially recognized and sanctioned agencies, and not necessarily on the basis of free associability. Hence the frequent importance of official parties, trade unions and the like, and the sanctions often used against unofficial and unrecognized groups.[17]

"Pluralism" may also exist in Latin America, but it is usually a system of limited pluralism, not the freewheeling laissez-faire pluralism of Tocqueville and the United States. Plural groups are often structured and controlled: an infinite multitude of uncontrolled groups "out there" would not do. To be accepted as one of the groups permitted to bargain in the political process, more than an informal, *ad hoc* association is required. Often, acceptance requires official licensing by the state and, hence, limitations on the group's activities.[18]

What *"democracy"* means in the Iberic–Latin American context is treated more fully in the next section. Suffice it here to suggest that while democracy is honored in Latin America, and while it has been established in come countries in some time periods, it, too, represents more an ideal to strive for than an operating reality. Further, "democratic government" is not necessarily incompatible with elitist rule and

---

16. Howard J. Wiarda, *Corporatism and Development: The Portuguese Experience* (Amherst: University of Massachusetts Press, 1977). More generally, see Wiarda, "Toward a Framework for the Study of Political Change in the Iberic-Latin Tradition: The Corporative Model," *World Politics*, January 1973, pp. 206-235, and Frederick Pike and Thomas Stritch, eds., *The New Corporatism: Social and Political Structures in the Iberian World* (Notre Dame, Ind.: University of Notre Dame Press, 1974).

17. Howard J. Wiarda, "The Corporative Origins of the Iberian and Latin American Labor Relations Systems," *Studies in Comparative International Development*, Spring 1978.

18. Juan Linz, "An Authoritarian Regime: Spain," in E. Allardt and Y. Littunen, eds., *Cleavages, Ideologies and Party Systems* (Helsinki: Academic Bookstore, 1964), pp. 291-341. In an otherwise provocative article, Philippe Schmitter has confused the issue by presenting corporatism and pluralism as polar opposites, when in fact pluralism may exist in corporatist or liberal polities. ("Still the Century of Corporatism?" in Pike and Stritch, eds.)

a hierarchical, pyramidal, non-egalitarian structure of society and polity.[19]

It is clear from the foregoing that the measure of democracy and human rights commonly applied to Latin America are strongly culture-bound. They derive largely from the Anglo-American constitutional model, which is often far-removed from Latin American culture and reality. Indeed, what such indices purport to measure—democracy—is not being measured at all. Instead, what is actually measured is the presence or absence of North American institutional molds in Latin America. By such criteria, Latin America naturally shows glaring deficiencies. To my mind, not only are the measures faulty, but the questions raised are the wrong ones. A set of measures which seeks to assess Latin American democracy on its own terms, rather than by North American criteria, and which (it is hoped) does begin to pose the right questions, is offered in the following section.

Before condemning the earlier indices to the ash can of anachronism and ethnocentrism, however, it should be said that the old measures do have some relevance for Latin America. For probably all the Latin American nations in fact represent a blend of both the corporatist-organicist-patrimonialist features highlighted here and the liberal, republican, representative features of the Anglo-American model. There are, then, two sets of institutional pillars on which the Iberic and Latin American state systems rest. Sometimes fused, sometimes parallel (but usually untouching), these two institutional foundations continue to coexist.[20] Any attempt to describe or measure Latin American democracy, therefore, must take both traditions into consideration; and the criteria one uses must reflect the composite, sometimes hodgepodge mix of historical organicist concepts and the newer liberal-democratic ones.

Toward New Definitions

Given the differences outlined above, let us proceed to new definitions of democracy and human rights in Latin America, taking into account

19. As derived from Roman law and Thomas Aquinas, as well as from modern secular theorists (Gumplowicz, Mosca, Pareto, Michels). See the discussion in Howard J. Wiarda, "Corporatist Theory and Ideology: A Latin American Development Paradigm," *Journal of Church and State*, Winter 1978.

20. John J. Bailey, "Pluralist and Corporatist Dimensions of Interest Representation in Colombia," in James Malloy, ed., *Authoritarianism and Corporatism in Latin America* (Pittsburgh: University of Pittsburgh Press, 1977); J. A. Morris and S. C. Ropp, "Corporatism and Dependent Development: A Honduran Case Study," *Latin American Research Review*, no. 12, 1977, pp. 27-68; Linn A. Hammergren, "Corporatism in Latin American Politics: A Reexamination of the Unique Tradition," *Comparative Politics*, July 1977, pp. 443-461; as well as Howard J. Wiarda, "Corporatism in Iberian and Latin American Political Analysis: Criticisms, Qualifications and the Context and 'Whys,'" *Comparative Politics*, January 1978, pp. 307-312.

(a) the distinctive features of the Iberic–Latin American political tradition and (b) the newer fusions. The following model has been fashioned in the form of a set of measurable indicators substitutable for the Fitzgibbon indices and based more on indigenous Latin American than on North American criteria. These new indices provide a means of measuring Latin American democracy on its own terms and also constitute a handy checklist to determine when a government oversteps its democratic legitimacy and is therefore likely to be challenged or overthrown. It must be recalled that the model presented is an ideal-typical construct, and that a fuller exposition would be required to account for the considerable variations among countries and within countries over time.

1. Strong, personalist, executive leadership, caudillo or Bonapartist rule, is not only permissible but expected. The president may rule in an authoritarian fashion but not a totalitarian one. He should be strong and paternalistic but not a tyrant. The president is only partially limited by a separate congress, judiciary or constitution; equally important in checking unbridled authority are the corporate group rights, or *fueros*, and the restraints imposed by moral law. By "moral law" is meant not the vague pragmatism of "situational ethics" but a higher eternal and natural law as articulated in Christian doctrine or in somewhat more secularized standards of "right" behavior, beyond which strong leaders may not go. The index one uses to measure the limits on presidential power, then, must take into account the widespread acceptability of authoritarian, paternalistic rule, as well as the fine line that often distinguishes authoritarianism from the unacceptable forms of tyranny and totalitarianism.[21]

2. Although the principle of separate, coequal branches of government has not been so firmly established or desired in Latin America as in the United States, it does exist. The congress is not coequal, but it does have important advisory, consultative and representative roles, corresponding to the historical functions of the traditional Córtes. The executive may be dominant, but the congress can still make life difficult for him; and if he rules entirely without a parliament, he runs the risk of alienating public opinion.[22]

The same applies to a government that rides roughshod over its national court system. Any government that comes to power, especially if it does so by extraconstitutional means, must immediately resolve its legitimacy problem. No court can entirely frustrate a government determined to pursue a particular action and willing to

21. Linz (see fn. 18, above) has most clearly drawn the authoritarian-totalitarian distinction.

22. W. Agor, *Latin American Legislatures* (New York: Praeger, 1971).

use force to accomplish it. Much less would any court interpose itself to prevent an armed insurrection aimed at overthrowing an existing government. However, judicial review and a functioning court system, although circumscribed, do often serve as checks on unbridled executive rule. Furthermore, the courts have a certain power in their ability to confer legitimacy on de facto regimes. A court may issue accords legitimating a regime in return for promises to observe human rights, to preserve or restore the constitution, or even to maintain the independence of the judiciary itself. Governments of doubtful legitimacy can thus be nudged toward a greater commitment to respect constitutional rights, although, of course, broad political support for such moves is also necessary.[23] Hence, while the principle of separate and coequal power among the three branches is not always an established or accepted principle of Latin American government, the courts and congress do have some autonomy and power. An index that measures these relations in terms of the Latin American conception of the role and functions of the courts and congress, rather than in terms of the North American view, would be both useful and feasible.

3. Free speech, free press and free assembly are also principles of Latin American constitutionalism, but they can similarly be limited for the "common good." Freedom is not an absolute but implies, to a far greater degree than in the United States, pre-determined bounds. Nor should one mistake the formal constitutional enactment of such rights, designed as goals and aspirations rather than operating realities, for their implementation. In addition, the laws and constitutions of Latin America give the executive broad discretionary power to declare a state of siege in times of emergency and suspend the usual guarantees. These emergency powers, however, are not intended to extend to violations of the human person. Nonetheless, the terrible centrifugal forces that have torn, and continue to tear, these societies apart are such that in Latin American constitutional law, political rights that might otherwise seem inviolable must legitimately give way before the need to preserve the state itself.

At the same time, the Latin American nations are signatories to a number of international documents for the protection of human rights. These documents include the UN Charter, the Universal Declaration of Human Rights, the Charter of the Organization of American States, and others. They encompass political and human rights (fair trial, habeas corpus, freedom of speech, etc.) and socioeconomic rights (work, food, health care, etc.). Further, although liberalism and republicanism—and the basic liberties usually associated with them—

23. Keith Rosenn, "Judicial Review in Latin America," *Ohio State Law Journal*, vol. 35, no. 4, 1974, pp. 785-819.

are still probably a minority strain in Latin America, the force of this tradition is nonetheless important and cannot be ignored. Finally, if it is inappropriate to judge the human rights credentials of various Latin American govenments by U.S. criteria, one may employ their own criteria. A case in point is Paraguay, where a state of emergency has been in effect almost continuously since 1947. Clearly, in this case, the emergency laws are being abused to maintain in power an unpopular authoritarian regime, to take measures that are disproportionate to the actual emergency, and to violate systematically the human rights of the opposition. Here, it would seem particularly appropriate for the United States to join the Paraguayan Bar Association in its formal condemnation of the continued abuse of the emergency laws.[24] For here it is clear that both by North American and Paraguayan criteria, human rights have been grossly violated.

4. Although the Latin American tradition provides for strong, centralized rule with little power given over to local government, a history of respect for the rights of local, state or regional entities also exists. Frequently such local rights are enshrined in long-standing charters, sometimes in the constitution itself, providing for varying degrees of autonomy from the central government. There are numerous center/periphery issues revolving around the autonomy question, perhaps most dramatically expressed in present-day Spain in the conflict over Basque and Catalan aspirations for independence from national policy emanating from Madrid. In Brazil, the centralization of power at the expense of state prerogatives involves a related issue; so do the Peruvian government's efforts to extend its control over the more isolated interior.[25] This conflict between center and periphery constitutes one of the major arenas of Latin American politics, although posed in this way, the issue is somewhat different from that posed by those North American scholars who have elevated the strength of representative government at the grassroots level to an index of democracy. To the extent a Latin American government respects local or regional *fueros*, it is considered "democratic"; when it rides roughshod over local rights and fails to care for those living in the periphery, it risks losing its democratic legitimacy.

5. Closely related to the issue of local and regional rights is the matter of corporate group rights. While few Latin American executives are strongly restrained by congressional or judicial limits on their power, they are "checked" by the major "power contenders" that are a

24. The Paraguayan document is reprinted in Karst and Rosenn, pp. 235ff. See also, Héctor Fix Zamudio, "Latin American Procedures for the Protection of the Individual," *Journal of the International Commission of Jurists*, December 1968, pp. 60-95.

25. Karst and Rosenn, introduction. Also see Hammergren.

part of their respective systems. These groups, the *fuerzas vivas* or *intereses creados*, include the army, the Church, economic elites, organized labor, the government bureaucracy, university students, and some others. These are not merely interest groups, in the U.S. sense, but fundamental vertebrae or corporate pillars on which the entire governmental superstructure rests. The concept is more a feudal, semifuedal or traditional Luso-Hispanic conception than it is a reflection of North American interest group pluralism.[26]

Any president who comes to power in Latin America must respect the autonomy, as expressed in his nation's charters and organic laws, of the several corporate pillars on which the government—any government—rests. This implies a certain respect (a) for the Church and the concordat (if any exists) between the state and the Vatican; (b) for the national university and its charter of autonomy; (c) for landed, commercial and industrial interests; and, perhaps above all, (d) for the armed forces and their privileged position as ultimate arbiters of national affairs, their special courts and immunities, and their direct access to policy through the *casa militar*. Any civilian president must be wary if he intervenes in the internal affairs of the military, for that is to invite the reverse process. Recently, corporate group rights have been extended to urban workers, peasants and women.

Obviously, the power of the various groups is unequal, helping to explain their differential treatment by the state. But generally, a government is considered democratic to the degree it respects the corporate group *fueros* of society's component units; to the extent it does not respect them, it not only violates basic rights but runs the risk of its own overthrow.[27]

6. A government is viewed as democratic to the degree that it is pluralistic and that all elements enjoy (a) autonomy from arbitrary authority and (b) considerable freedom of action and movement. By "pluralism" we mean not the laissez-faire hurly-burly of the largely unrestricted U.S. interest-group struggle, but a limited pluralism in which the various groups, while controlled and restricted by the state, often elaborately so, nonetheless enjoy a certain contractually defined independence from it.[28] A system is pluralistic in Latin America insofar as it allows or safeguards centers of power other than itself: the family;

26. Ronald C. Newton, "On 'Functional Groups,' 'Fragmentation,' and 'Pluralism' in Spanish American Political Society," *Hispanic American Historical Review*, February 1970, pp. 1-29.

27. Howard J. Wiarda and Harvey F. Kline, *Latin American Politics and Development* (Boston: Houghton-Mifflin, 1979), introduction.

28. See Linz; also, David Collier and Ruth Berins Collier, "Who Does What, to Whom, and How: Toward a Comparative Analysis of Latin American Corporatism," in Malloy, ed.

the local entity; the hacienda; various religious, cultural, educational, philanthropic and professional agencies; to say nothing of the municipal, regional and corporate groups already referred to, which promote the rights and interests of their members and protect them against unwarranted encroachments by the state or other groups. Some of these groups, such as the family, local community or the Church, are considered to be prior to the state, theoretically at least, both in history and in natural law. Except in emergencies (and even then there are some safeguards), these are sacrosanct institutions against which no government may move unless it is willing to sacrifice the loyalty and support of the group affected. A government that antagonizes several groups by violating their rights can be, and likely will be, overthrown.

7. Latin American governments are also obligated to protect the basic human rights of individual citizens. These individual rights are not necessarily conceived of in the same way or afforded the same elevated position as in the U.S. Constitution, although through such devices as the writ of *amparo, segurança,* habeas corpus and cassation, some protection is received. Even more fundamental, because it stems from natural law, is the obligation of government to leave people alone, to respect their individuality, to protect the inviolability of the human person. While authoritarian rule of a paternalistic sort may be permissible or even desired, a regime or police agency that terrorizes its own people is not. Torture and killings as instruments of state policy; turning loose the police or army on hapless trade unions, students or opposition elements; summary trials and executions; beating women, priests and children—all are clearly outside the bounds of acceptable behavior. The cumulative effect of such violations may undermine the legitimacy of a regime. Batista, Trujillo, Pérez Jiménez, Somoza and the present Chilean regime are cases in point; Brazil seems to be skirting the edge.[29]

8. Government must be both "representative" and "participatory," but in the Latin American sense of those terms. It must be representative of society, meaning those groups (the Church, army, labor, elites, etc.) that have been duly recognized by the state and given official sanction as legitimate power contenders in the system. These groups are usually represented in the cabinet, congress or council of state, and in the ministries and state agencies, and they have special access to the centers of decisionmaking. The state must also provide for participation, generally through an officially sanctioned network of associations for workers, farmers, women and so forth. To

29. See especially "Proceedings of the 67th Annual Meeting of the American Society of International Law," *American Journal of International Law,* November 1973, pp. 198-226.

the extent a government allows such representation and participation, it may be considered democratic; but to the extent it closes off or stifles such legitimate group life, it may lose its democratic standing. Note, however, that not all elements are represented in the scheme (unorganized peasants, Indians and urban "marginals" are excluded), nor is the principle of "one man, one vote" necessarily applicable.[30]

9. While government must be "democratic" in the sense I have been describing, that is not always incompatible with "top-down" or elitist rule. Pervasive notions of hierarchy and authority often imply that deference is given to those with a perceived "natural" right to rule. The elites, however, are obligated not to abuse their privileged position. They must provide charity and benefices to the poor and, while retaining social distance, respect the rights and individuality of those beneath them on the social scale. They may be patronizing and paternalistic, but they may not ignore or excessively disdain their workers, peasants or servants. Transferred to the national level, this means an obligation, also, to accommodate and absorb the rising social forces, not to close them out as in Nicaragua and Paraguay. In classic patron-client fashion—now extended from the hacienda to the state agency—the *patrón* enjoys a preponderance of rights, but the situation cannot be entirely one-way. The clients also have their rights, and a *patrón* or government that ignores or abuses those rights may lose the loyalty usually given in return for various favors. The cumulative loss of his clients' services and loyalty spells trouble for any *patrón*, including the great national *patrón*, the government itself.[31]

10. A new criterion for democratic legitimacy in Latin America includes the requirement that government provide for economic development and social justice. Development and social justice have become part of the ideology of the region and are closely linked to its concept of democracy. The older conception—that people must be poor, live in wretched housing and see their children diseased and with bloated bellies "because poverty is good for the soul," or because the Church obligated them to accept their station in life—is dead or dying. The "revolution of rising expectations" has come to Latin America, and any government must "deliver" in the way of housing, health services, food, jobs, etc.—or else! Democracy in Latin America has thus been redefined to encompass social and economic criteria as well as political ones—though the precise nature of the regime that brings social justice and economic growth is left open, and the models used (including varying forms of populism and syndicalism) may,

30. Wiarda, *Corporatism and Development...*, chaps. 2-4, 11.

31. Emilio Willems, *Latin American Culture: An Anthropological Synthesis* (New York: Harper & Row, 1975), chaps. 5, 14, 17.

again, be quite distinct from those of the United States or Western Europe.[32]

11. A Latin American government that oversteps the bounds of permissible behavior outlined above, rides roughshod over natural law and rights, concentrates all power in its own hands, violates the contracts and *fueros* governing corporate associational life, becomes brutal and oppressive—in short, a tyranny—deserves to fall. The right of rebellion is as much a part of the Latin American political tradition as is the obligation to obedience. Against an unjust tyrant the citizen has the right and duty to resist, to go outside the system, to seek to replace it. But even here, certain ground rules apply. Faced with widespread popular opposition, the tyrant has an obligation to resign (e.g., Perón, Batista) instead of seeking to stay in office and provoking further bloodshed. Such barbarism as napalming rural villages and unleashing campaigns of terror against the opposition has consistently been considered illegitimate and self-defeating. The opposition, however, is also obliged to play by the rules: the right of asylum for officials of the outgoing government must be respected; those who wish to go into exile should be allowed to do so; reprisals should be avoided. In short, the final measure of democracy in Latin America is the right to rebel against the system if that system becomes tyrannous, abusive and ineffective.[33]

Nowhere in the above list of characteristics and criteria for measuring democracy in Latin America is the notion of a formalized, constitutional separation of powers or checks and balances given central focus; nor do elections, political parties, and the like constitute the chief criteria. Of course, in some countries today and in others in the past, elections make a critical difference, but it must be re-emphasized that elections are not the only legitimate route to power and certainly do not, by themselves, constitute an adequate measure of democracy. The criteria developed here seek to go beyond the older, largely U.S.-based, procedural gauges of democracy and, rather than impose outside criteria, to develop criteria deriving from the context and tradition of the Latin American culture-area.

Yet, while the concepts and criteria developed here derive from what is even now probably the dominant tradition in Latin America, it is no longer the *only* one. For alongside the historical tradition—here

32. Charles W. Anderson et al., *Issues of Political Development*, 2nd ed. (Englewood Cliffs, N.J.: Prentice-Hall, 1974), pt. 3.

33. The literature on this theme is vast, ranging from Saint Thomas to Fidel Castro's "History Will Absolve Me." See also Manuel Giménez Fernández, *Las doctrinas populistas en la independencia de Hispanoamérica* (Seville: 1947), and Lawrence E. Rothstein, "Aquinas and Revolution," a paper presented at the Annual Meeting of the American Political Science Association, Chicago, September 2-5, 1976.

briefly characterized as organicist, patrimonialist and corporatist (in the broad, political-cultural sense)—there has grown a genuinely liberal-democratic one. These two models (which give rise to the "two Spains" concept, for instance) may coexist within a given country, sometimes wholly separate and sometimes overlapping, considerably complicating any measurement of democracy in Latin America. The situation is complicated further (in Peru, Portugal, Cuba) by the superimposition of a third, socialist overlay. Any assessment of democracy's presence or absence in Latin America must keep in mind the distinctive historical-cultural meaning of democracy in the area as well as the newer conceptions that have recently emerged.

Needed: Care, Caution and Sensitivity

This discussion began with the question of whether democracy and human rights are everywhere the same and universal. The answer as applied to Iberia and Latin America is both yes and no. Neither the nations of Latin America nor Spain and Portugal have much trouble agreeing with the human rights principles set forth in various international charters; and there was probably no hypocrisy in King Juan Carlos's message to the U.S. Congress that his goal was to "perfect" Spanish democracy, or in Ernesto Geisel's labeling Brazil a "relative democracy." At the same time, one must be cognizant of the impact of what Lucian Pye once termed the "world culture,"[34] largely Western, which forces dependent countries like those in Latin America to redefine themselves in our terms instead of their own historical ones, to be judged by our criteria of democracy and human rights whether or not they wish to be and whether or not the Western notion is even functional in their own distinct political culture.

It is clear from this discussion that in Iberia and Latin America, key terms like "representation," "participation," "pluralism," "democracy" and "rights" frequently have quite different meanings, carry different connotations, or imply different expectations from those predominant in the Anglo-American context. One must bear in mind the hierarchy and differential importance of distinct bodies of law in Latin America, that human rights (*derechos*) may occupy a different level of importance than in U.S. law, that individual human rights are often subordinated to corporate group rights (*fueros*), and that human and group rights may both be subordinated to the common good or the necessity of maintaining the unity and integrity of the state.

34. In Lucian Pye and Sidney Verba, eds., *Political Culture and Political Development* (Princeton, N.J.: Princeton University Press, 1965), introduction.

The sweep of the analysis given here is broad, and the model presented is an ideal-typical one. It is a heuristic device and is not meant to correspond to reality in every instance. That, however, should not blind us to the numerous qualifiers and variations that must be recognized. At one level, a "macro" model such as this is useful as a means of alerting us to the general parameters of a major issue-area, but for specific policy recommendations, we must also take into account variations within nations, between nations and across time. A dynamic component must be incorporated so that the model is less deterministic than it sometimes appears.[35] We must be alerted to the human rights-versus-intervention dilemma, and we must weigh carefully the mechanisms that produce successes in our efforts to promote human rights and those that produce backfires. We must further distinguish among types of human rights: (a) those involving freedom from government violation of the person, (b) social and economic rights and (c) democratic political freedoms. On the first of these types, there exists considerable international consensus; hence, it may be hypothesized, there is some possibility of policy success in the human rights area. On the second, which lies at the heart of the acrimonious "North-South" dispute, and which involves the issues of who has primary responsibility for resolving socioeconomic ills and how best to achieve that goal, there is less consensus; hence, there is probably less chance of success. On the third category (the main topic of discussion here), there is even less agreement and probably an even slimmer chance of success.

I conclude with a series of caveats. We must, I think, be skeptical of U.S. journalists and government officials who insist on interpreting Latin American democracy entirely through their own cultural and political concepts. The "liberalizing" and "democratizing" currents and "struggles" of which they so frequently write or speak are often valid up to a point, but they tend to be based on superficial readings derived from North American, rather than Latin American, criteria. The fact that political parties exist in Spain, for example, and that elections are held is insufficient evidence on which to describe Spain as democratic. But the reverse also holds. Because the Latin American systems do not always correspond to U.S. notions of democracy, we have frequently been quick to brand them as "failures." The fact is that in many cases they are simply practicing a type of "democracy" that is reflective more of their own historical and cultural understanding of that term than of the Anglo-American conception.

35. These more dynamic features of change and modernization are treated in some of my writings: "Toward a Framework...," *Politics and Social Change...*, and *Transcending Corporatism? The Portuguese Corporative System and the Revolution of 1974* (Columbia: University of South Carolina, Institute of International Studies, 1976).

So, too, with human rights. What is a violation of human rights in one cultural context may not be in another, or may be seen in a different light, or may have another meaning altogether. Furthermore, over time, these conceptions may change along with broader developmental changes, thus giving human rights a different meaning in one epoch or in one group of countries than in another. The *fuero*, for instance, will mean something different as the particular group grows in strength or as the balance between the competing groups is altered. Hence, in the case of "democracy" and "human rights," a conception is needed that derives from Latin American understandings and not from our own culture-biased views. The concepts discussed here represent a first step in that direction. We must distinguish between (a) what the United States conceives of as human rights violations (which often become issues reflective primarily of U.S. domestic politics) and (b) those violations that reflect actual Latin American disenchantment with their own governments' actions. Care, caution and sensitivity to the cultural and political differences involved are required. These qualities can lead us to a greater understanding of how the Latin American political systems actually function, and can keep us from despair when Latin American politics evolve in directions that do not correspond to our own conception of democracy.

We can and should be in favor of democracy and human rights in Latin America (and at home) while also differentiating among the several categories of human rights, understanding how they apply in various countries at different stages of development, and remaining sensitive to differences of meaning and interpretation in societies other than our own. We cannot impose our conceptions on nations where human rights and democracy are conceived of differently without considerable damage being done to them and to us. We must come to grips with the fact that distinct culture-areas have different understandings of democratic concepts and their relative importance.[36] The criteria of democracy and human rights offered here give us a handle to grasp, a means to support human rights while also being sensitive to cultural differences. Hence, for the policymaker as well as the scholar the same caveats apply: prudence, discretion, empathy and a sophisticated understanding of quite different social and political traditions.[37]

36. Fortunately, there are signs that those responsible for policy have begun to grasp these differences. See, for example, the speeches of Cyrus R. Vance ("Human Rights Policy") and Warren Christopher ("Human Rights: Principle and Realism"), both available from the U.S. Department of State, Bureau of Public Affairs, Office of Media Service.
37. Sound policy and informed moral judgment must be based on a clear understanding of the broad cultural differences extant. A thorough, factual dossier on democracy and human rights in specific countries is also required. This article helps provide a theoretical understanding of the issues involved and thus serves as a necessary prelude

For if we are to cease acting as "policeman to the world," we probably cannot, unless with great modesty, circumspection and sensitivity, presume to be its political and moral superior either.

---

to policy; Department of State reports and reports growing out of congressional hearings on human rights in specific countries provide the essential data base.

For policymakers who may have already grasped the distinct conceptions involved and who have the factual materials at hand, however, the dilemma is no longer a lack of understanding but what to do about governments that violate democratic norms and human rights even on their own indigenous terms. What levers can be manipulated? What mechanisms are appropriate? How can human rights and democracy be encouraged without unwarranted interference in another nation's internal affairs?—these issues must constitute the subject matter of a separate paper.

The United States Government's Commitment to Human Rights

RICHARD SCHIFTER

What I shall try to do today is to share with you my views as to the substantive issues with which we must deal in formulating a United States human rights policy, as distinct from the slogans and public-relations stances to which we have been exposed.

One of the reasons why much of the recent public debate over the issue of human rights has been both confused and confusing is that the questions on which there may very well be overwhelming consensus have not been clearly separated from those over which there is indeed controversy. Before delving into the human rights debate, it is, therefore, important to distinguish between ultimate objectives and the methods to be used in reaching them.

As to ultimate objectives, few of us will doubt that the great majority of Americans will at all times support the proposition that our concern for human rights must and should be an important factor in our relations with other countries. Americans are compassionate. We, as a people, care about human rights and human dignity. We object to and disapprove of violations of human rights, wherever they might occur.

Moreover, let us keep in mind, that fatalism is not a national character of ours. We believe that when things go wrong, they should be set right and that we, as a nation, should, at least, try to help set them right.

It follows that as a country which believes in human rights, we expect our government to reflect that belief in all its actions, both domestic and foreign. It is also worth keeping in mind that in our

NOTE: Presentation made to the Council of the Americas and reprinted from the *Congressional Record—Senate* (June 25, 1981) S7196-97.

53

country, more than in many others, basic popular attitudes on foreign policy register on the government and are reflected in its policies. The basic American concern for human rights will indeed be taken into account by the government, irrespective of what administration might be in power. That is so because, first, the policymakers are not a self-segregated elite, but an integral part of the American people whose sentiments they share.

Beyond that the policymakers are politicians and, as such, tend to reflect the prevailing view of the electorate. As a matter of fact, if we want to look for a prototype of the American concerned with human rights and committed to human decency, embodying the essential goodness of the American character, we can easily start with the head of the work force at 1600 Pennsylvania Avenue. And indeed, since last January, the new Administration's basic commitment to the cause of human rights has been stated and restated by the President, the Vice President, and the Secretary of State.

To be sure, the broad majority consensus on human rights of which I have spoken focuses only on basic principles, on ultimate goals. It generally does not deal with the question of methods that the Government of the United States may adopt to reach these goals.

It is when we get to the questions of detail in the execution of policy that we enter the realm of controversy. There may be arguments as to which particular approach is best designed to achieve a desired result. There may also be arguments as to the manner in which the human rights policy must be correlated with other foreign policy objectives. It is in this area, the area of tactics, that we find changes in approach as we go from administration to administration and it is in that area that we also run into heated debates among advocates of differing approaches.

I would suggest, on the basis of my experience of recent months, that in analyzing the problem of how to carry out a human rights policy, we should distinguish between two broad categories of issues on which our Government might be asked to act. A UNESCO committee on which I recently served recognized this distinction by labeling one category as "questions."

A "case" involves a single individual or a limited group of named individuals who have been or are threatened to be deprived of a human right and for whom specific relief is being sought, such as the commutation of a death sentence or the release from prison.

The term "question," by contrast, was an abbreviation of the phrase "questions of massive, systematic or flagrant violations of human rights which result either from a policy contrary to human rights...or from an accumulation of individual cases forming a con-

54

sistent pattern." The relief that is sought when we deal with a "question" is for the accused government to change its basic mode of conducting its affairs. It does not take a great deal of experience in the conduct of international affairs to recognize that as difficult as it may be to obtain a favorable solution to a "case," it is far more difficult to obtain the desired answer to a "question."

It stands to reason that once the United States decides to use its good offices on behalf of a victim of a human rights violation, it should adopt a course of action which is most likely to attain the desired result of relief for the victim. There are few who will disagree that to attain that result the best initial approach is one of quiet diplomacy. That does not mean that private groups should not focus their attention on a specific human rights violation and speak out on that subject. But a government should generally seek to avoid painting another government into a corner. The latter might find it easier to bow to world public opinion than to give in to the demands of another national government. Bowing to world public opinion can be explained away as an act of generosity performed for the sake of maintaining international good-will. For one country to submit to the demand of another tends to wound national pride and would be viewed as an act of vassalage.

What a government may not want to say to another government in public, it can, however, say in private. Private communication is not only less embarrassing, but it can also be more precise. Public statements can easily be embellished by the media, both in the country from which the communication originates and the one to which it is directed. Such embellishment can easily exacerbate the problem. Also, the public communication can, as recent history has shown, be designed for its public-relations effect in the dispatching country, which may very well be inversely proportional to its effectiveness in attaining the desired result in the receiving country. One of your publications [Council of the Americas], issued last year, made this precise point. Here is how you put it:

"Certain unilateral actions by the U.S. Government have hampered the effectiveness of the U.S. corporations vis-à-vis their foreign competitors, cost the U.S. economy jobs, and hurt the nation's balance of payments. At the same time, these actions have not achieved the desired political result in Latin America."

The question can, of course, appropriately be asked as to how the general public will find out that representations have been, in fact, made on a human rights issue, if it is done in a confidential setting. The answer is that because of the very fact that representations have been made in private, it will not be possible to publicize the matter. All that an outsider will be able to do is examine the pattern of behavior of certain countries over a period of time, see what improvements in the field of human rights can be recognized and try to draw inferences therefrom.

For example, would it not be reasonable to assume that the commutation of the death sentence of Kim Dae Jung, as well as the recent amnesty in South Korea, were among the topics of conversation between South Korean and American official representatives before the South Koreans acted? Would it not be reasonable to make similar assumptions with regard to certain actions taken by the Government of Argentina?

Does that mean that we should under no circumstances go public with an appeal for life or the freedom of a person who is a victim of a human rights violation? It does not mean that at all. It does mean that we should go public only as a last resort, when it is clear that all other methods have failed.

I have, you will note, not made any distinction in the foregoing discussion between friendly, neutral, and unfriendly countries. The same basic principles apply. It is indeed a well-known fact that quiet diplomacy has helped us obtain the release from imprisonment of some Soviet dissidents.

Now let us turn to what the UNESCO committee to which I referred earlier calls "questions," patterns of conduct by governments which have the effect of depriving large numbers of people of their human rights.

What is it that our country should do where such a pattern emerges? Should we there, too, try our best at private diplomacy? Under what circumstances should we go public? Should we, in making representations, consider the circumstances under which a government acts, namely whether it is suppressing peaceful dissent or whether it is confronted by terrorism and armed rebellion? Should we take a country's geopolitical importance to the United States into account, before acting on that country's human rights record?

Here, at last, some observers might say, we have reached the core of the present controversy, the basic difference between the Carter Administration and the Reagan Administration. The former, they might contend, adopted a purist human rights policy. The latter, by contrast, they say, is prepared to sacrifice human rights for geopolitics.

On further examination, I submit, you will find that it ain't necessarily so. As I am speaking to you today as a private citizen and not as an official of the State Department, let me be less than diplomatic and cite two specific cases. As we all know, we have not made a major issue of the human rights record of the People's Republic of China, not during the Carter years and not since then. We have seen the wave of democratization which crested in 1976 recede. We have refrained from public criticism not for lack of sympathy for the brave souls who came forward a few years ago to put posters on Democracy Wall but because we did not think it was in our national interest to speak up. Nor have we made a major public issue of the status of women in Saudi Arabia, not in the Carter years, and not since then.

What I have thus suggested is that relating our human rights policy to other foreign policy concerns and then acting on the basis of what we consider to be in our national interest is not a new approach invented by the Reagan Administration. It is a perfectly understandable and wholly defensible aspect of our conduct of foreign affairs.

The critical question has been to determine where our national interests lie. Key policymakers in the past Administration appear to have been of the view that our position on the international scene would not be adversely affected if we lost the friendship of some Latin American governments which we considered to be human rights violators. President Carter, you will recall, spoke in 1977 approvingly of the end of the inordinate fear of Communism.

The present Administration does not consider that fear inordinate, but reasonably justified by the Soviet Union's record in world affairs. Nor does the Administration feel sanguine about our own margin of safety. There is, therefore, a far less cavalier attitude about our losing the friendship of countries in the Western Hemisphere that would like to maintain good relations with us or permitting a government not friendly to the Soviet Union to be replaced by one which looks to Moscow for guidance.

While Latin America is the region that comes to mind when we speak of the Carter Administration's willingness to lose friends, sight is often lost of the fact that there is another part of the world where a poorly thought-through policy did serious harm to American interests. Considerations of human rights violations caused us, in 1977, to terminate our military relationship to Ethiopia, which then caused the Ethiopian government to switch to the Soviet side. It can, you will agree, fairly be said that conditions of human rights in that country have not improved as a result of the entrenchment in Addis Ababa of Soviet, Cuban, and East German military detachments or technical advisers.

Our experience with Ethiopia does indeed bring into sharp focus the geopolitical problems we face. Without our having registered a gain for the cause of human rights, we now find the Soviet Union thoroughly established on the Horn of Africa, in an improved position to endanger our lifeline to the Persian Gulf. For when we speak of the steps we need to take to safeguard our national interests, we are referring principally to our concern over the imperialist, expansionist designs of the Soviet Union, the threat posed by the Soviet Union to its immediate neighbors, to our access to national resources vital to our economy, and to the cause of freedom.

The fact that I have put the cause of freedom last does not mean that it should be regarded least important. The United States was deeply concerned about the fact that the Soviet Union was a totalitarian police state long before the Soviets were able to endanger American access to our vital resources. As we all know, in country after country that has been absorbed into the Soviet bloc, Soviet domination has meant the abrogation of the most basic human freedoms, the establishment of control of the people by a secret police force and the suppression, and often killing or imprisonment, of all those who stand in the way of the new regime.

Thus, when we give weight to considerations of national interest in formulating our policy toward an independent country which is guilty of human rights violations, we are by no means betraying the cause of human rights. What we are doing, at worst, is subordinating certain perfectly legitimate short-range human rights concerns to our effort to protect the free world against the most serious long-term threat to the cause of human rights.

What I have emphasized from the very beginning of this presentation is that human rights violations are a matter of concern to us wherever and whenever they occur. The difficult problem with which we must deal is what it is that our Government can do about these violations when we are not focusing on an individual case in which we are asking for clemency but are urging a change in the basic pattern of a government's conduct. That is indeed the setting when we should use quiet diplomacy in speaking to our friends but should speak out loud in calling attention to the pattern of conduct in those countries which are not friendly.

Here again, our actions should be guided by our purpose to obtain beneficial results for the human rights cause. Getting a government to change its pattern of conduct as a result of outside intervention will under no circumstances be easy. But when we are dealing with a friendly or potentially friendly country, the chances of success would be greatest if we engage in off-the-record discussions, discussions which take into full account the problem the country might face, such as terrorism or armed rebellion, and the existence or non-existence of institutions on which civil order can be built.

The situation is obviously different when we deal with the Soviet Union and countries in the Soviet bloc. As distinct from the individual case in which clemency might be brought about through quiet diplomacy, informal discussions by United States representatives with Soviet or Soviet-allied officials will not succeed in eradicating Stalinist practices in the post-Stalin Soviet sphere. If there is any hope of change, it stems from the possibility that the Soviet Union or its satellites will be shamed into such change by world public opinion or by those peaceful dissidents who will have persevered in speaking out because they knew they were not abandoned, that there were people elsewhere who identified with their cause.

Is there, you might ask, a risk that our raising these human rights issues vis-à-vis the Soviet Union might endanger world peace? I submit to you that there is no historic evidence that our abstention from strong criticism of Soviet domestic policy will significantly affect that country's pursuit of its foreign policy objectives. It is from the pinnacle of the United States–Soviet friendship at the end of World War II, after we had time and again averted our eyes from the brutally repressive actions of the Soviet regime, that Stalin set the course for the takeover of Eastern Europe. Conversely, our repeated condemnations of Soviet aggression and Soviet repression since the invasion of Afghanistan have not prevented Leonid Brezhnev from speaking in measured tones to the West in his most recent foreign policy statements.

Not only will our expression of concern with the Soviet Union's human rights record not do any harm to our relations with that country, but in the long run we have indeed reason to hope that it might do good. What the history of post-Stalin Russia, post-Mao China and now post-Gierek Poland has demonstrated is that not even the most brutal repressive measures can entirely extinguish the spark of the instinctive human longing to be free.

Orwellian language is indeed spoken in many countries but the Orwellian nightmare of 1984 has not come true, for the efforts at brainwashing entire populations have fortunately utterly failed. What is important, though, is that we keep up the spirit of those who have the courage to speak out for the rights of man in repressive totalitarian societies. It is important that they know that their efforts at peaceful change to a freer system are recognized, applauded and supported. It is, for that reason, that where we can do little or nothing to obtain immediate changes for the better, where there is no opportunity to obtain results through quiet diplomacy, we speak out, and by doing so keep the flame of hope burning bright.

The Timerman Case

MARK FALCOFF

One morning in April 1977, twenty armed men in civilian clothes, claiming to be under orders from the Tenth Infantry Brigade of the Argentine army, invaded the Buenos Aires apartment of a well-known newspaper publisher and editor named Jacobo Timerman. Captured and blindfolded, Timerman was pushed onto the rear floor of an automobile, and led off to what subsequently became six months of solitary confinement, interrupted only by occasional trips to the toilet, meals, and sessions with an electrical torture-shock device. In September, he was brought before a War Council, that is, a military court, still uninformed of the charges against him. After a fourteen-hour session in which Timerman was pointedly questioned about every aspect of his life, work, political activities, and Jewish identity, the council ruled that there was no reason to hold him under arrest. This decision was reached late in the month, and communicated to the prisoner in his cell in mid-October.

However, instead of releasing him, the Argentine military government transferred him to house arrest for two additional years. In September 1979, the Argentine Supreme Court convened to consider Timerman's case, and for the second time found no grounds for his continued detainment. The high command of the army met and voted nonetheless that Timerman should remain imprisoned, preferably in a military garrison, and added gratuitously that the entire Supreme Court should resign for having arrived at their finding. Only when Argentine President General Jorge Videla threatened to resign himself was Timerman released, but, apparently as part of a compromise worked out with his fellow generals, the President ordered the publisher stripped of his property and his Argentine citizenship, and permanently expelled from his country. Today he lives in Tel Aviv, although he is a frequent visitor to the United States, where he has become—if one can countenance such macabre usage—a "human rights celebrity." One of his most recent appearances in that capacity was as a silent witness-for-the-prosecution in the Senate confirmation hearings of Ernest W. Lefever, President Reagan's then-nominee to be Assistant Secretary of State for Human Rights and Humanitarian Affairs.

Timerman's accession to international prominence is not surprising, for his case was the subject of worldwide concern and protest, involving at various times representatives in Argentina of the United States, Israel, and the Vatican, as well as various Jewish and non-Jewish humanitarian organizations. Indeed, few political prisoners in Argentina (or elsewhere) have been so fortunate in the range and importance of the friends who have rushed to their defense, and few of those friends, sad to say, have been as successful elsewhere. Now, however, Timerman is free to speak on his own, and he has done so in a book recently published under the title *Prisoner Without a Name, Cell Without a Number.*[1]

The appearance of Timerman's book and a renewed controversy in the Senate and the public prints over U.S. human-rights policy may be nothing more than a coincidence, but the earliest reviews have not let the opportunity pass without comment. John Leonard in the New York *Times* (May 7, 1981) led off with the really breathtaking assertion that Timerman's testament establishes that "Argentina is no more civilized than the Soviet Union, Iran, or Uganda," and that what the publisher confronted there in 1977 was nothing less than "Nazism."

Leonard's colleague Anthony Lewis has been no less hyperbolic. In a front-page article in the Times Sunday *Book Review* (May 10, 1981), Lewis discusses the Timerman book under 50-point letters spelling out "THE FINAL SOLUTION IN ARGENTINA." In the body of the article, however, some agendas slightly different from those of Timerman himself are brought forward for our consideration:

> The methods of modern tyranny [Lewis writes] repeat themselves. With this reality compare the political-science abstraction that has served since last January 20 as a premise of United States human-rights policy: the theory that right-wing governments are merely "authoritarian" and do less damage to human rights than "totalitarian" regimes.
>
> The principal author of that theory is Jeane Kirkpatrick, United States Ambassador to the United Nations. Elaborating on it in 1979 in the magazine *Commentary*, she wrote that, unlike Communists, "traditional autocrats" observe "traditional taboos." For example, they respect "habitual patterns of family and personal relations."

1. Knopf, 164 pp., $10.95.

I thought about Ambassador Kirkpatrick when I read Timerman's description of the Miralles family: father, two sons, and a daughter-in-law. Timerman heard they were tortured, and they were not the only ones.

What Timerman is describing, Lewis concludes, is "our century's special contribution to civilization: state terrorism." And for those slow to perceive what water is being drawn to whose mill, the Kirkus Service review of the Timerman book puts it baldly: "In heated, sometimes striving prose...is inscribed a Jeremiah-an lament, furious and sad...*and especially timely now that the U.S. is again cozying up to Argentina*" (emphasis added).

Q.E.D. The Timerman case "establishes" (a) that there are no differences between right-wing authoritarian states and Communist regimes; (b) that the Reagan administration is therefore hypocritical and two-faced in its moral standards; and (c) that the horrors in Timerman's book represent a fair sample of everyday life in "autocratic" regimes which Washington is now said to prefer in many Third World countries, regimes which—to judge, anyway, from the headlines of the Lewis article—are morally (and presumably even statistically?) comparable to Nazi Germany; and (d) in Argentina it has been the state which has constituted the real terrorist threat.

But if Timerman's book is to serve as a propaganda windfall for the foreign-policy establishment of the American Left, the leaders of that movement had best hope that most people confine their knowledge of the case to what reviewers say about it. It would not do to have too many people actually *read* Timerman's account. For within the confines of this slim volume (only 164 pages), there is a good deal more than a record of the author's travails at the hands of various police sadists, torturers, and military megalomaniacs. In fact, roughly half the text covers other matters. These include Timerman's autobiography, a discussion of Argentine politics between 1966 and 1973 (the date of Perón's return), and, most important of all, some remarkably revealing glimpses of military politics in the period between the overthrow of Perón's successor-spouse (1976) and Timerman's release three years later.

One might assume, charitably, that the reason most reviewers have chosen not to dwell upon (or in some cases, even mention) this half of *Prisoner* is that they themselves do not quite understand some of these complexities, and that, in any event, they are not relevant to the issue of human rights. But let us not be ingenuous: there are some embarrassing pieces of information in this book, from which Lewis and Company would be best advised to protect their special constituencies. Even a careful reader with no particular knowledge of the Argentine setting is bound to be puzzled and perhaps even troubled by certain apparent paradoxes and incongruities in the narrative.[2]

The truth is that Timerman drops some rather tantalizing leads in his autobiographical pages, but probably not one American in several million is in a position to pick these up and make complete sense out of them. For to assemble these fragments coherently, one must know something about a host of recondite topics—Peronism and anti-Peronism, anti-Semitism in Argentina, the role of that country's armed forces, the nature of politics in the second Perón period, and not least, the ways open to a penniless immigrant boy from Russia to rise to wealth and influence in a remote yet sophisticated South American society.

The central drama around which Timerman's story actually revolves is the return in 1973 of former President Juan Perón after nearly two decades in exile. In a metaphorical sense, this was not an event which occurred all at once, but from the late 1960's on it could be predicted—barring the demise of its protagonist—with increasing assurance. For during the fifteen or so years following Perón's overthrow in 1955, the Argentine economy continued to register, and with accumulating force, the decline which had begun during the late years of his presidency, and increasing numbers of citizens were coming to "remember" his regime (1946–55) in terms of the prosperity which had, however, actually been an accidental byproduct of a postwar boom in agricultural commodity prices. At the same time, Perón's populist approach to income redistribution (from which he had been withdrawing in the final two years of this period) had bequeathed to Argentina a trade-union movement firmly loyal to the deposed leader, an organized working class which at its lowest point represented about one-third of the electorate.

During these years all manner of experiments were launched to ease Argentine politics into a post-Peronist era: a civilian, democratic government determined to wean Perón's followers from his person (Frondizi, 1958–62); a civilian government elected under a complicated system which effectively disenfranchised Peronist voters (Illia, 1963–66); and a succession of military presidencies aimed at promoting economic development as a substitute for politics itself (Generals Onganía, Levingston, Lanusse, 1966–73). Alas, neither by persuasion

2. This was the case of Eliot Fremont-Smith, who reviewed the book for the *Village Voice* ("Killing Jews," May 13–19, 1981). To his credit, Fremont-Smith brought his doubts to the surface, noting the particular paradox of the "Nazi state" being provisioned by Israeli arms.

nor by force could the ghost be exorcised.

What was perhaps equally to the point, at the very same time an entire generation was coming to maturity which knew of Perón only what could be evoked from childhood memories (and sometimes, not even those) or conveyed by parental recall. In the picture of the vanished regime which came to dominate the imagination of these young people, the most appealing feature was probably its vaunted "anti-imperialism" and "independent" (i.e., anti-American) foreign policy. The fact that Perón's challenge to the United States was more bluster than reality was somehow overlooked, and of course the unflagging devotion of the working class enveloped the exiled leader in a retrospective glamour which quelled any lingering doubts. Thus by 1970, Perón found himself being courted by groups which had stood apart from his first regime and even actively opposed it—leftist students and Marxist intellectuals. Unlike the Argentine Left of the 1940's and 1950's, however, this successor generation had added to its Marxist breviaries the writings of Ché Guevara, Frantz Fanon, Muammar Qaddafi, and other heterodox sources, whose only common feature was a predilection for violence and direct action.

The role which this new Peronist "Left" played was utterly crucial to the decision of the Argentine armed forces to relinquish power to an elected government. For from 1970 on, paramilitary formations nominally loyal to Perón, such as the Montoneros or the People's Revolutionary Army (ERP), began to assassinate prominent military personalities, including one former president. They also began to accumulate, through a chain of kidnappings and bank robberies, a treasury which rivaled the assets of any multinational corporation. Already blamed by the public for their inability to turn the economy around, the generals now found themselves humiliated by their apparent impotence in the face of a challenge from rank amateurs, who in the bargain were blighting the fruits of power. What, after all, was the point in holding a provincial governorship if one did not physically survive one's term?

One mark of the isolation in which the military found itself by the early 1970's was the degree to which the civilian opposition in Argentina responded to the escalating violence of urban guerrillas by proffering somewhat limp "sociological" explanations. On this subject, Timerman is especially scathing:

> Juan Domingo Perón used to say that "Violence from above engenders violence from below"—a statement that could be found in any Harvard, MIT, or Hudson Institute study on the aggressive feelings of populations with meager resources. A liberal statement, a sociological equation, which in an organ-

ized country might lead merely to a polemic on the ways in which such aggressiveness can be eliminated through housing, education, or public-health programs.

In Argentina, however, Peronist youth understood at once what Perón was saying: he approved of violence and terrorism, and would lend his support to any murder, kidnapping, or assault that fit into his goals for the reconquest of power . . . .

Anyone opposed to the tactical methods established by Perón would be executed by the boys, pushed from below by the violence from above.

The "violence from above" disguised as the "violence from below," however, did its work, and by 1973 the resistance of the generals was broken. Perón was allowed to return for a week's visit, although not to run for the presidency. In March, a stand-in for Perón, Héctor Cámpora, was elected, and in May, the Peronists formally returned to power. After a scant three months, during which he revealed himself to be the captive of the Peronist Left, Cámpora was ordered by Perón to resign and convoke new elections in which the great man could run on his own. Perón returned to Argentina in June, and in September was re-elected with a thumping 62 percent of the vote. A month later, nearly eighty years old, he walked back into the Government House he had abandoned in disgrace nearly twenty years before.

In spite of the overwhelming endorsement he had received from the electorate, Perón could not inaugurate an era of peace and concord; too many different expectations had been raised by his return. The Left, of course, expected him to reveal himself as a Marxist, and in truth, Perón had done an excellent job of stringing these people along (and using them) during his late years of exile. But—quite apart from Perón's record, his personality, and his most intimate views—this was hardly a likely eventuality. For the largest element supporting his return was a "traditional" following which was populist rather than Marxist. That is, it favored a style of government which combined personalism, state capitalism, gangsterism, and bread-and-butter unionism with a rather haphazard showering of social-welfare benefits on the "loyal," rather than a systematic restructuring of Argentine society along more egalitarian lines. The ranks of traditional Peronism included everything from right-wing Catholics to trade-union militants, from industrialists to provincial intellectuals; this, after all, was precisely the constituency which Perón had represented during his first period of power. All the talk about "national liberation" and "Third World" solidarity was a later addition, and represented (as Perón well knew) far fewer votes.

As long as he was but a distant hope, Perón could inspire the loyalty of both wings. Once in power he was forced to choose, and choose he did: first, by selecting as his Vice President his wife, María Estela ("Isabel"), generally identified with the traditionalist wing; and then, several months after his inauguration, by officially inviting the Left to subsume itself into his movement of class collaboration and national recontruction (as he called it), or depart.

Even before this confrontation, however, elements of the Peronist Left, unable to slacken a disposition to combat which had been wound to feverish intensity, were at war with the regime they had helped to install. Their peremptory dismissal by Perón at a public ceremony only provided a new reason to persist in their acts of violence. And then, after Perón's death in July 1974, the guerrillas launched an all-out offensive, assuming that they would be the inevitable beneficiaries of the fall of his incompetent spouse.

This was not, however, the case. For the guerrillas were quickly joined by a bewildering variety of contending forces in what became a sort of civil war in miniature. These included, in Timerman's description,

> rural and urban Trotskyite guerrillas; right-wing Peronist death squads; armed terrorist groups of the large labor unions, used for handling union matters; paramilitary army groups, dedicated to avenging the murder of their men; para-police groups of both the Left and the Right vying for supremacy within the organization of federal and provincial police forces; and terrorist groups of Catholic rightists organized by cabals who opposed Pope John XXIII's proposals to reconcile the liberal leftist Catholic priests seeking to apply—generally, with anarchistic zeal—the ideological thesis of rapprochement between the Church and the poor.

To which he adds that

> these, of course, were only the principal groups of *organized* or systematized violence. Hundreds of other organizations involved in the eroticism of violence existed, small units that found ideological justification for armed struggle in a poem by Neruda or an essay by Marcuse. Lefebre might be as useful as Heidegger; a few lines by Mao Zedong might trigger off the assassination of a businessman in a Buenos Aires suburb; and a hazy interpretation of Mircea Eliade might be perfect for kidnapping an industrialist to obtain a ransom that would make possible a further perusal of Indian philosophy and

mysticism to corroborate the importance of national liberation.

The far Left and the far Right came to employ similar tactics, indeed, at times, the very same tactics. The Montoneros, Timerman reports, succeeded in "forcing five hundred large business firms to pay a monthly protection sum against kidnapping or assault of their executives." The Triple A—a right-wing terrorist organization— obtained a copy of this list and forced "these five hundred large firms to subscribe to its financial support. The companies thus [paid] both organizations." Timerman does not say so, but extrapolating from events of this sort elsewhere in Latin America, it is not implausible that the Triple A obtained the Montoneros' list because some members of one group were also members of the other.

It was to put an end to this situation that the Argentine military, under Army Commander General Jorge Rafael Videla, overthrew the government of Isabel Perón on March 24, 1976. The record shows that this act was endorsed by the broadest spectrum of political forces in Argentina, including one of the most influential and prestigious newspapers in the country, *La Opinión*, edited by one Jacobo Timerman.

About this remarkable newspaper Timerman has very little to say, and what he tells us is not always true. He remarks that it was often likened to *Le Monde*, but "in relation to the ideological position of the French daily, one could say that *La Opinión* was a typically liberal newspaper." While the veracity of this statement depends entirely upon how one defines "liberal," the comparison with *Le Monde* seems more exact, since *La Opinión* was a newspaper of very high editorial quality which frequently made up what it did not know. Further, like its French counterpart, it combined a vague sort of international and cultural leftism with an elegant anti-Americanism—a Gaullism, as it were, packaged for Argentine consumption. All of which amounts to saying something which Timerman flatly denies—that *La Opinión* was (or at any rate, soon became after its founding in 1971) a Peronist newspaper.[3] In any case, it could hardly have been anything else. To

3. One serious difference between *Le Monde* and *La Opinión* was that the latter never carried on a flirtation with the Palestinians. But—quite apart from Timerman's own heritage and commitments—this was not a particularly heterodox position for a newspaper in the Peronist mainstream. Perón himself had always been moderately friendly to Israel, and in fact during his presidency, 1973–74, Argentine delegations generally refused to subscribe to "anti-Zionist" resolutions retailed at the United Nations and at conferences of the "nonaligned."

start a newspaper is no idle enterprise, particularly in a country like Argentina, for an immigrant with no family ties to the leading banking families. Quite apart from credit, it requires advertising, and on this score Timerman is utterly candid: *La Opinión* could not have survived without large blocks of space taken by public-sector enterprises, which in Argentina represent a very significant portion of the industrial plant, and whose publicity budgets equip any government with a marvelous tool for influencing the tone of the press.[4]

But Timerman's Peronism was not wholly mercenary: he was convinced, as were so many Argentine professionals, businessmen, and intellectuals who read his paper, that only Perón could reconcile the pressing agendas of nationalism, redistribution, economic growth, civilian government, and social peace. Nor was his shift to favoring a military coup in 1976 necessarily inspired by dishonorable motives; his paper simply reflected the general flow of Argentine opinion, which after Perón's death, the revealed incompetence of his successor, and the unremitting threnody of terrorist violence, came to despair of a civilian political solution.

Thus the picture of a Jewish liberal democrat editing something like the old New York *Post* in Buenos Aires is very, very wide of the mark; *that* sort of liberalism holds no appeal for Argentines, and Timerman would have been a far less clever man had he propagated it. If Timerman's liberal admirers in the United States were able to read the back numbers of his newspaper, rather than to accept at face value what he himself says about it, they might be no less determined to protest his arrest and treatment in captivity, but somewhat more skeptical of his claims to represent their values.

The question inevitably arises: if Timerman was so successful in negotiating—and indeed, turning to his own benefit—the shifting currents of Argentine politics, why, then, was he arrested at all? Here, too, *Prisoner* tells us what at best is only part of the truth.

After the coup which deposed Isabel Perón, the military initiated a sweep of known or suspected elements of the violent Left. As is necessarily the case in any urban setting where the forces of order must contend with the virtual invisibility of the enemy, a blanket repression is often the only means which offers any hope of success. In such

4. It has been reported that Timerman's "excellent connections" in the government and the labor unions made it possible for him to compel the German-language daily *Argentinisches Tageblatt* to print *La Opinión* for four years below cost, a figure estimated in 1975 to represent $40,000 a month. See Benno Weiser Varon, "Don't Rescue Latin American Jews," *Midstream*, December 1980.

situations—let us not mince words—the distinction between terrorist and suspect, between sympathizer and activist, indeed, between innocent and guilty, is often lost—but in the end the job can be done, if the will is there to do it.

This is precisely what the Montoneros and the ERP never expected, forgetting (if they ever knew) that army officers are not vacillating liberals, and that with every kidnapping, murder, and bombing, the guerrillas themselves were untying the last cords of professional military restraint.[5] In his book, Timerman describes in moving terms his own gradual disillusionment with this process, which was very far from what he had in mind in supporting the coup ("to terminate the violence of both the Left and Right . . . to curb terrorism through legal channels"), a disillusionment which, he says, led him to begin systematically publishing the names of *desaparecidos* (literally, "persons who have disappeared"; persons abducted without due process), until his newspaper was shut down and he himself joined the ranks of Argentina's growing army of political prisoners.

What he does not mention, however, is a little episode which occurred in early April 1977—that is to say, about the time of his arrest. A young Argentine Jewish banker with connections in Belgian and American financial circles, by the name of David Graiver—who happened to be Timerman's principal partner in the ownership of *La Opinión*—was forced to declare the bankruptcy of his New York operations, which centered around the American Bank and Trust Company. Graiver himself is alleged to have died shortly thereafter in a mysterious plane crash in Mexico. The rest of the story, reported at the time by leading journals in the United States, has been told by a former Israeli diplomat with broad experience in South America:

> Graiver's wife. . . returned from Mexico to Buenos Aires in order to liquidate her husband's Argentinian holdings. One day, she received an unannounced visit from Colonel Camps, chief of police of the Province of [Buenos Aires]. The Colonel and those who accompanied him did not wear their uniforms, but Mrs. Graiver recognized their military gait and made a fateful mistake. "But we have to let you know," she said, "that you have nothing to worry about! Your money is safe!" She believed she was speaking to a delegation of the Montoneros, the country's strongest and wealthiest guerrilla movement. Colonel Camps perked up his ears: what money was Mrs. Graiver speaking about?. . .

5. Perhaps indeed there were some Left guerrillas who imagined that by provoking wholesale repression, the Argentine population would be properly "radicalized" and eventually respond to a call for a general uprising. If so, they were profoundly mistaken.

[The Montoneros, it appeared, had] picked Graiver as their secret investment broker. Why Graiver? They had been "in business" with him—they had kidnapped his son and had received his ransom.

[With this apparent discovery], all members of the Graiver family, including his parents, were arrested. And so was, on April 15, 1977, a business partner of David Graiver—Jacobo Timerman. Guilt by association? To the military mind it did not seem far-fetched that Timerman should have known of the Graiver-Montoneros connection.[6]

Understandably, Timerman has no desire to raise this matter; in fact, he prefers not to discuss it at all. But he has provided some rather convincing indirect evidence that it is far from irrelevant. During his recent trip to the United States, when pressed to explain his connections with Graiver by a generally sympathetic interviewer for the *Wall Street Journal*, the best Timerman could manage was the statement: "The questions you are asking me...these are the questions they were asking me when I was tortured." Just so.[7]

The Graiver piece of the puzzle fits admirably well with the next, which Timerman *does* provide—namely, an account of the extraordinary conflict and confusion which his case provoked within the highest ranks of the Argentine army. On one level, it was by no means clear that Timerman was guilty of subversive activities, a caveat which carried considerable weight with President Videla. On another, Timerman had excellent connections with the highest ranks of the military— so much so, in fact, that had his enemies within the high command not prevailed, the defense counsel at his "trial" would have been none other than Lieutenant General Alejandro Lanusse, a member of one of the nation's most socially distinguished families, and President of Argentina from 1971 to 1973! On yet another, Timerman admits that in his own mind he was never sure President Videla even knew about plans to arrest him until it was too late.

Why, then, did not the President merely recognize that an error had been made and rectify it by signing a release order, or, at the very least assure Timerman of the benefits of due process? The answer to that question is extraordinarily interesting, and Timerman does not hesitate to give it. After the fall of Isabel Perón, each intelligence branch of the armed forces undertook its own counter-guerrilla operation. Various military leaders became, in Timerman's telling, virtual warlords in zones under their control, "whereupon the chaotic, an-

6. Varon, *op. cit.*

7. Seth Lipsky, "A Conversation with Publisher Jacobo Timerman," *Wall Street Journal*, June 4, 1981.

archistic terrorism of the Left and of the fascist death squads gave way to intrinsic, systematized, rationally planned terrorism." But this was not a development that occurred without difficulty, for over the question of how to carry out counter-guerrilla operations the Argentine military leadership split into two factions—"moderates" and "extremists."

The "moderates"—the term, please note, is Timerman's, not Ambassador Kirkpatrick's or my own—"strove to accomplish peaceful acts. . . . They were, are, and will always be opposed to all excesses." The problem was that "the moderates of the military revolution had. . . been unable to gain control over repression or over, in many instances, the official operation of parallel justice." Timerman believes that he was kidnapped by the "extremist" sector of the army, but that, far from approving the act, President Videla and (now President, then Army Commander) General Roberto Viola "tried to convert my disappearance into an arrest in order to save my life."

One can, of course, deplore the inability of Generals Videla and Viola to master the situation effectively, and even comprehend the obloquy to which both men have been subjected in the Western liberal press; after all, with whom else could one inquire after the fate of Timerman save the duly constituted and diplomatically recognized authorities? And yet. . . . Although as his book winds to its close Timerman uses ever more frequently the term "Nazi" to describe the present Argentine state, his description of its inner workings evokes not the memoirs of Albert Speer but a ramshackle Balkan kingdom designed by Borges or Kafka. Here Timerman was, a political prisoner in a country whose president and army commander were fairly good personal friends of his, two generals whose own position in the tangled web of military politics required them to pretend to be less concerned over Timerman's fate than they really were; both men had to defend before world opinion and multilateral diplomatic inquiry an abduction of which they did not approve; and finally, they had to utilize the lever of international pressure so as to appear "forced" to do what they undoubtedly wished to do anyway, but not in so humiliating a fashion as to lose all credibility before their fellow officers.

While Timerman remained under house arrest, a complicated series of negotiations was carried out in barracks and service clubs, in suburban villas and in the windowless buildings that housed the various intelligence services. In the end General Videla just barely survived the process; forty-eight hours after Timerman's release, the government had to quell a military uprising in the city of Córdoba, led by "extremists" bitterly disappointed at the result.

In all of these events, to expect no appearance whatever of the "Jewish question" would simply be too much to hope for. But if Timerman offers some chilling insights into the nature of Argentine anti-Semitism, he does not resolve very clearly whether his Jewish identity was a particularly wounding misfortune, or the secret amulet which saved his life. Or rather, he holds out both possibilities, which, for all their untidiness side by side, probably comes closest to the truth. But let us take this matter by parts.

It is certainly true that anti-Semitism exists in Argentina, although precisely *how* serious a problem it is cannot be fixed with certainty. Even Argentina's Jews themselves, who should be the leading experts on the subject, have never been able to agree; outsiders therefore can only offer impressions. In certain ways it might be said that the contemporary position of Jews in that country resembles that of the community in the United States during the 1920's. Comparisons of this sort are of course inevitably imperfect: for example, Argentine universities are free of restrictive admissions practices; even the most luxurious hotels and resorts do not generally refuse admission to Jews; and Jews may live in any neighborhood in which they can afford to rent or buy. Withal, there is still considerable social and business discrimination which nonetheless has not prevented some outstanding individuals (Timerman among them) from making their way to the top. Perhaps the United States in 1929 or 1935, but not Germany—in 1934 or any time thereafter.

This still leaves plenty to discuss and deplore, but again, one must define clearly the boundaries of the subject. The political culture of the extreme Right in Argentina has always included anti-Semitism, but in spite of that country's many military governments since 1930, these people have had surprisingly little influence on the welfare (or lack of it) of the Jewish community. Instead, they have languished in a curious cul-de-sac of "historical institutes," little magazines, musty parish houses, and, in recent times, in right-wing "action" groups and among certain formations of the police. For these people, miraculously preserved in the spiritual atmosphere of the year 1937, Communism, Zionism, labor unions, free love, and Hollywood films are all of a piece, and nothing which has happened in the last two decades, not even the international campaign against Israel orchestrated by the Communist bloc, has attracted their notice. These are the people into whose hands Timerman had the misfortune to fall during his first six months of confinement, and it was their residual influence at the higher ranks of the military which imparted the specifically anti-Semitic overtones to his trial (though not, it must be emphasized, to the actual outcome of that event).

But if the far Right in Argentina has failed to discern the difference between Communism and Zionism, the extreme Left has not, and this notwithstanding the fact that quite a few extreme Left groups have harbored Jewish members. Among the Montoneros, the ERP, and their analogues, as Timerman acutely observes, "hatred of the Jew adds a spicy and delicious ingredient into the struggle for World Revolution." To which he adds, with extraordinary insight, that

> the Jew can satisfy [the] quota of irrational hatred required by every human being but which systematized ideology such as the extreme Left is unable to acknowledge in its relationship with society. Therefore, why not leave the window open, at least a crack, to allow that hatred to filter in? And against whom else if not the Jew?

This is more than a literary point, since Timerman reveals that, prior to his abduction, he had received death threats from both groups—on one occasion, in the same day's mail—and that he remains convinced to this day that if the Left had managed to seize power in Argentina, "I would have been placed against the wall and shot, following a summary trial. The charge: counterrevolutionary Zionism."

Does the fact that he fell into the hands of the extreme Right rather than the extreme Left make any difference? It would seem so. In Timerman's telling, there are no palms of mercy to be distributed among his captors, since he believes they spared his life only because they had decided he could be more useful alive, "confessing" leftist Zionist connections with left-wing Argentine terrorism. Then, at last, these people would be granted the pogrom that so many previous military regimes had denied them.

Perhaps this is indeed an accurate reconstruction of the mind-set of his tormentors. But note: *no such connection was established.* The military court was compelled to dismiss the charges against Timerman, and meanwhile an international campaign enlisting the support of such august personages as the President of the United States and the Pope put sufficient pressure on the Argentine government to effect Timerman's eventual release. It is not a frivolous exercise to speculate upon what constellation of forces, domestic and foreign, would have been capable of restraining the hands of the ERP had they been successful in *their* plans to abduct him.

Meanwhile, what was happening beyond the prison gates? This question is utterly crucial, for upon it hinges the precise political nature of

73

the military regime. At times Timerman resorts to metaphors used to describe typically totalitarian societies—people paralyzed by fear, afraid to acknowledge even their best friends should the latter fall afoul of the Machine. But at other times, and rather more often, it seems to me, he suggests that whatever his own difficulties (and those of his fellow prisoners) life in the world outside simply went on much as it always had—and with few exceptions, the business community, the press, the political parties, and other civic forces willingly accepted the stewardship of the military, excesses and all, as a costly but necessary sacrifice.

This version is of course less flattering to his countrymen than the first, but it is also pregnant with an embarrassing possibility—that in spite of the wave of right-wing terror centered in certain places of detention, *in Argentine society as a whole* the regime confined its interests to peace and public order (as it chose to define them, of course) rather than extending them to a reshaping of institutions along totalitarian lines. This still did not make that country an object worthy of admiration by liberal democrats in 1977, but for most Argentines, including, it must be said, one of the largest Jewish communities in the world, it was not an intolerable place to live.

This last piece of information is very inconvenient, for how can what Timerman repeatedly refers to as a resurrection of the "Nazi state" permit Jews not only to exist within its borders, but even to prosper? To resolve this contradiction, he introduces a bizarre concept which might be described as Holocaust-by-Installments, a notion which also allows him to ventilate all of his resentments against the organized Jewish community in Argentina. Here are some samples of his reasoning:

> The point of reference for the Jewish leaders of Buenos Aires, as for Jewish leaders in many parts of the world, is the horror of the Holocaust. . . .
>
> For me, the point of reference is equally the responsibility of Jews in the face of any anti-Semitic act. The point of reference is Jewish action; the Jewish silence of the Hitler years towards Hitler's acts.
>
> I was never able to understand how the horrors of the Holocaust could diminish the significance of the violation of Jewish girls in clandestine Argentine prisons. . . .
>
> To my mind, always the incorporation of the Holocaust into my life meant never to allow the Argentine police to feel that they were authorized to humiliate Jewish prisoners. *I never imagined that there would be Jewish leaders who would utilize the horrors of the Holocaust to maintain that the most advantageous response to certain anti-Semitic aggressions of a much less brutal nature was silence* [emphasis added].

From this tendentious point—of which more below—Timerman jumps to a comparison between the Jews of Argentina and the German Jewish community in 1938. Needless to say, the former do not come out very well, their leaders likened to the Judenräte of Nazi-occupied Europe, that tragic mechanism by which the Germans during World War II utilized existing Jewish bodies to organize the transshipment of their co-religionists to "the East," never to return.

But is this in fact what has been going on in Argentina during the last five or six years? It is true that, as Timerman says, "the Argentine military, as in Germany, has seized banks, business firms, jewelry, properties, and furnishing belonging to persecuted Jews." He does not mention, however, that the same regime has confiscated the assets of "persecuted Gentiles." For the truth is that the criterion of "persecution" has not been ethnic identity but subversion, real or imagined. This makes life no more pleasant for the "persecuted" (many of whom were actually guilty, however wrongly treated they have been from a judicial point of view), but it introduces a massive distinction which Timerman has no right to blur.

Nor is it a fact that the Argentine military is systematically—or unsystematically, for that matter—eradicating the Jewish population of that country. It should be unnecessary to have to say this, but none of the mechanisms associated with the Holocaust, including forced identification, racial "passports," restrictions on professional and economic life, exclusion from educational institutions, much less forced labor camps or extermination centers—is in operation or formation. The Jewish Agency and a large Israeli diplomatic mission pursue their activities unobstructed, indeed indirectly assisted by the host government. Nor are Jews who wish to emigrate to Israel, the United States, or elsewhere prohibited from departing with all of their property intact and their liquid assets freely convertible into any currency.

This still leaves much to be desired in the lives of those who remain (as the leaders whom Timerman attacks for their "silence" have been the first to admit), and it may well be that those who have fallen afoul of the forces of order have consistently suffered, as Timerman claims, with redoubled intensity because of the fact that they are Jewish. Police brutality toward prisoners, whether inspired by racial hatred or ideological differences, is always worth protesting, but it serves no useful purpose to distort the true dimensions of the problem: it cheapens the lives of those exterminated in Central and Eastern Europe, while doing less than nothing to alleviate the suffering of those political prisoners in Argentina who happen to be Jewish.

This still leaves the *pièce de résistance*: the statement attributed by Timerman to Dr. Nehemias Reznitsky, president of the political umbrella organization of the Argentine Jewish community, that not all anti-Semitic acts ought to be protested, "for that would create a confrontation with highly powerful sectors of the army. There was a better tactic: to protest some and maintain silence over others, in an attempt to negotiate and survive." On this point, Dr. Reznitsky will have to have his own day in court. But perhaps an outsider may be permitted this one observation: some of the Jews arrested in the anti-guerrilla campaign did in fact have connections with the violent Left. Others were legitimate objects of suspicion. Still others were innocent. Can the leaders of the Jewish community be faulted for respecting these differences and proceeding on each case according to its separate merits? In a society with a functioning judicial system and civilian control of the police, the process would require fewer compromises and less tortured maneuvering. But the breakdown of civilian government in Argentina was not the fault of either the generals or the Jews; and if some of the latter suffered at the hands of some of the former, the ultimate responsibility lies not with the leadership of the Jewish community, but with those anxious, neurotic young men and women who—in Timerman's words—converted "terrorism and violence" into "the sole creative potential, the sole imaginative, emotional, erotic expression of a nation."

Let us try to do the sums of this remarkably complex problem. Jacobo Timerman was not kidnapped because he was a Jew, or probably even because he was protesting the conduct of Argentina's security forces, but because his business partner was discovered to have intimate connections with one of the most important left-wing guerrilla organizations in the country. Although innocent, Timerman was treated with unspeakable cruelty for about six months, undergoing a process which was all the harsher because of the outspoken anti-Semitism of his captors. He was not, however, a great defender of liberal democratic values (who in Argentina in those days was?) and he was not brought to trial for that reason. Rather, Timerman was an exceptionally able political speculator who had played his game with remarkable agility until an accidental revelation pushed him off his balance and sent him into the maelstrom of terror and counter-terror which followed the death of Perón. His experiences in Argentine prisons reveal the mistreatment of Jewish prisoners because they are Jewish, but his book does not establish—not by ten country miles—that people are arrested because they are Jewish. No "final solution" is under way in Argentina.

Now it would be unconscionable for this reason to minimize in any way the personal suffering which Timerman underwent. To any prisoner a place of detention is a totalitarian society by definition, and Timerman's more than most: in one of the very few moments of black humor in an otherwise uniformly depressing book, he describes the "national security school" in which inmates, guards, and orderlies all sat side-by-side, diligently pursuing the three R's of "anti-Communism." If for Timerman the difference between an authoritarian and totalitarian government was not immediately apparent, he can certainly be forgiven. Still and all, there was no show trial at which he confessed a guilt which was not his, and in the end he was in fact released.

Where does this leave the rest of us? Foreign-policy decisions are always exercises in choice, for Americans usually between unpalatable alternatives. It was precisely to assist in those difficult choices that Jeane Kirkpatrick tried to formulate in these pages (she did not and could not have "invented") the distinction between two completely different kinds of dictatorship.[8] The key to that difference was not how regimes treated their political prisoners, but where the boundaries of the jail were located. In societies like Cuba or the German Democratic Republic, the prison walls are virtually coterminous with the nation's geographical limits, and when a door is suddenly pushed ajar (as it was at the Peruvian embassy in Havana last year) countless thousands react precisely the way that convicts could be expected to respond in a similar situation—they stampede unceremoniously to freedom.

Countries like Argentina are different, and the difference begins with the fact that they have no "boat people." Whatever horrors occur in the places of confinement (and the proper response to these is neither complacency nor rationalization), in the very texture of life, wide areas of personal, spiritual, and political and economic freedom are allowed to persist and expand. It is unfortunate, to say the very least, to have to measure the "improvement" of human rights in that society (or any like it) by cataloguing the annually decreasing number of violations, but that diminishing statistic is still a sign of progress—and of hope. One longs for such auspicious auguries from societies which the liberal press thinks more worthy of our conciliatory efforts.

There will always be a difference of opinion over the most effective method of protesting cases such as Timerman's, but simply to label an authoritarian military regime as virtually indistinguishable from something it is not—namely, a totalitarian state along Nazi or Soviet lines—is to write off several thousand political prisoners, harden the

8. "Dictatorships and Double Standards," *Commentary*, November 1979.

determination of their captors to resist outside pressures on their behalf, and consign the resolution of matters to an eventuality which is not about to occur—a foreign invasion of Argentina to depose the existing authorities and open the jails.[9]

In an emotional outburst published in the *Times* (May 17, 1981) several days after his review of Timerman's book, Anthony Lewis returned to the subject by insisting that our relations with Argentina turned about the question of "our own soul." Are things at such a point, he asked, "that we Americans must enlist torturers and murderers as allies, and proclaim their values, their God, as ours?...What kind of country are we?" We are this kind of country: one that must balance our highest ideals against the world we find outside our borders, a world in which most other nations, including the sanctimonious Swedes and the hypocritical French, ask no questions as long as they can make a sale; a country which is locked in a struggle of incalculable consequence with a major world power that is also, as Anthony Lewis well knows, courting the same men he refers to as "torturers and murderers."

If the sole purpose of foreign policy were to make us feel good about ourselves, we could gladly concede the Soviets their Argentine prize; in practice, however, even Jimmy Carter concluded that this was a luxury we could not afford. If our Argentine options are both nearly (but not *precisely*) equally repugnant, the blame should be placed squarely upon the shoulders of those to whom it belongs—not our elected officials, but those Argentines ("alienated youth," "Third World" priests, leftist gangsters, and irresponsible politicians) who narrowed the range of possibilities by destroying their country's only civilian, democratic option (with all its warts) in nearly a generation, bringing to the surface a subcutaneous culture of police brutality and anti-Semitism which could well have remained where it was for an indefinite period.

That is the real significance of the Timerman case, and one can only hope that some day the point will be grasped as firmly in the editorial offices of Washington and New York as it already is in Buenos Aires.

9. In an op-ed page article endorsing Timerman's portrait of Argentina's rulers and calling the regime there "a new kind of totalitarianism," Robert Cox, editor-in-chief of the Buenos Aires *Herald* actually goes on to describe something very nearly the opposite of totalitarian rule: "If labels must be applied, Argentina could best be described as feudalistic and anarchic....The tragedy stems from the fact that central authority, and the responsibility that goes with it, has never been established by the moderates in the military..."(New York *Times*, June 9, 1981). Here then is yet another, if perhaps inadvertent, confirmation of the usefulness of the distinction.

Human Rights
and Whited Sepulchres

Michael Novak

One of the most misused and dangerous notions of recent years, a notion by now reduced to a mere slogan, is human rights. The concept itself is a sacred one, and like any sacred concept, its misuse or overuse trivializes it. At least three fundamental mistakes are being made about human rights in contemporary discourse. First, too many people designate human rights without designating corresponding obligations. If there is no one to fulfill such obligations, then the alleged human right has no substance; it is merely a form of words. For example, if you say that every human being has a right to food, you must say who has the obligation to supply that food. If you state that homosexuals have a right to teach young children, then you are also asserting that other persons have an obligation, even perhaps against their own will, to yield to that right. If you say that every person has a right to a job, then at least by implication you are stating that someone—probably the state—has an obligation to supply a job, presumably even by coercion if necessary.

Rights do not come free. Each right has a corresponding cost. When a great many things are asserted as a matter of right, then there comes into existence a kind of hierarchy of rights. Asserted of too many things, the word "right" becomes empty of meaning. Indeed, people often seem to use it to express something that they devoutly wish might be the case.

Second, the notion of human rights is often used to describe a public proclamation or a respectful moral attitude. Thus, commentators sometimes appeal to the leaders of nations to "respect the human rights" of their subjects. This seems to suggest that these leaders should change their moral attitudes. But this is not the notion

NOTE: Keynote address, Human Rights Conference, Kalamazoo College, Kalamazoo, Michigan, April 26, 1978.

79

of human rights established by *The Federalist* or our own Bill of Rights. According to "the new science of politics" that Hamilton and Madison believed they had discovered, the expression "human rights" had an institutional meaning, not merely a moral meaning. Human rights, Madison suggested, are not worth the paper they are written on unless there are established institutions in which claims to such rights can be adjudicated and unless there are, as well, established interests and parties within such institutions able and willing to compete to establish such rights. The real defense of human rights does not lie in words on paper, or even in moral sentiments among leaders, or in the moral sentiments of the population as a whole. The real defense of human rights—indeed, their substantive reality—is constituted by access to institutions in which the exponents of competing rights can legally and fairly contend. Thus, in the Soviet Union, all sorts of human rights have been announced on paper. Indeed, Soviet leaders often pay oral respect to the concept of human rights. But no parties or factions are allowed to exist that might openly compete for the settlement of rights, and no institutions exist in which the fairness and impartiality of such procedures might be established. Unfortunately, in most of the world, human rights seem to consist of proclamations on paper and of ritualized moral attitudes. In only a few countries have human rights been institutionalized.

Third, the very concept of human rights only makes sense within a certain kind of intellectual and cultural history. Although the language and rhetoric of human rights have now become international—and virtually universal, as in the Universal Declaration of Human Rights—to a large extent these expressions merely borrow the esteem in which Western conceptions of human rights have come to be held, without borrowing either their conceptual framework or their institutional substance. In totalitarian states, the state is the source of all rights. It is not conceded that rights inhere in individual persons. Institutions that might mediate the rights of individuals either do not exist or do not have power against the state. The language of human rights is used. But it has no reality. Only if you believe that the individual conscience is inviolable and that each individual human being is an originating source of sovereignty, agency, and resistance to the state can you even have a concept of human rights that is more than mere words. In those traditions in which the state is the originating source of all power and all rights, the concept of human rights has been reduced to mere rhetoric. The state, or at least the leadership cadre of the state, has total rights. Apart from these rights, the individual human being has no legal standing. In such circumstances, no theoretical contradiction is involved in simply exterminating individuals.

In short, we should be very careful in using the expression "human rights." To do so is to invoke a specific intellectual history, a specific set of philosophical and theological presuppositions, a specific set of historical institutions, and a specific set of interests and parties able to contend in defense of their rights and so to make them effective in the public sphere. In other words, to speak of rights is not to speak of pious proclamations. It is not to speak of venerable declarations in public documents. It is not to speak of fervent moral sentiments. It is not to speak of wishes or desires for a better world. It is to speak of limited moral claims on the part of some, entailing corresponding limited obligations on the part of others, as protected by interests and parties contending through public institutions of due process.

We frequently use the term "human rights" far more lightly than we should. We speak of every child's "right" to a good education, to clean air and clean water, to love and attention and food and drink and work and many other things besides. What we seem to mean by these declarations is that it would be "wrong"—that is, less than appropriate or desirable—for the child to be deprived of such goods. We confuse natural *goods* with natural *rights*. We might in the same sense say that every child has a right to heroism and to holiness, to saintliness and to moral perfection. We would then mean that every child has a capacity for such things and that it would be good if these capacities were fulfilled. But we truly do not expect to see moral perfection attained. As we cannot now expect to see moral perfection attained in the individual's moral life, so we also cannot expect to see all natural goods made perfectly available in actual societies.

Even when we speak, in more limited and sober terms, of "the right to life, liberty, and the pursuit of happiness," for example, we do not mean that each person will live forever, that total laissez faire is a right, or that each person will, or must, pursue his or her own happiness. We mean, rather, to limit the power of the state over such matters.

Finally, there is another confusion in the way we use these words today. President Carter drew the world's attention to a politics of human rights during his first few months in office. He did not do so in a political vacuum, however. Several years earlier, Senator Henry M. Jackson had already introduced the conception of human rights in international politics by his insistence that the United States might make concessions to the Soviet Union in the economic sphere only if, and in proportion as, the Soviets fulfilled institutionally their public declarations of human rights. Senator Jackson was trying to bring about decisive institutional changes in the structure of Soviet cultural life in exchange for American collaboration in building up Soviet economic life. Some years later, Daniel Patrick Moynihan, then ambassador to the United Nations, called upon the free world to take the ideological offensive and to establish before the minds of people everywhere the realities of Western concepts and Western institutions, to which some nations seemed to be committed only on paper. He wished to expose publicly an almost universal hypocrisy. He did so, he said quite frankly, as a political weapon. On the level of ideas, he said, the world is at war. A few nations believe in human rights, not only as basic concepts, but also as concrete, institutionalized procedures. Other nations believe in human rights only as mere words. For too long, he held, the party of liberty has tried to adjust its posture defensively, trying never to criticize, never to boast, never to advance, never to challenge. These defensive tactics have permitted others to hide behind Orwellian language and to claim in rhetoric what they had no intention of institutionalizing in practice. As ambassador to India, Moynihan had found this world situation deeply unfair; worse, it was a stark service to untruth. Simply for the sake of truth, he argued, we should start calling things by their names and force hypocrites to defend themselves. We should place the moral burden on them.

Beyond the issue of truth, Moynihan also saw an issue of political advantage. The job is worth doing for its own sake, but it is also worth doing for the sake of those in other places who wish to be freer than they are. By forcing the totalitarian nations, in particular, to face the gap between their rhetoric and their practice, one might hope to wring from them concessions and face-saving devices that might strengthen, at least by a little, the forces of dissent and genuine liberation within them.

The Carter administration turned this human rights policy inside out. It did not make human rights a policy of truth. It did not make human rights a policy of political advantage. It assumed a false position of objectivity and independence, as if in an Olympian way the United States stood outside the affairs of the rest of the world and looked down with judgment upon all nations. Thus, the Carter administration made an attempt to be "evenhanded" and to balance every accusation against an opponent of the United States with an accusation against a friend. In addition, it did not even raise the question of totalitarianism. It pretended that all nations erred against human rights more or less equally. No distinction was made between totalitarian nations and authoritarian nations.

The latter is one of the most important distinctions of our times. There are many cases of authoritarian nations that have become democratic. There are no cases of totalitarian nations that have become democratic.

It is not easy for nations to achieve liberty. In the entire history of the human race, only a very few nations have done so. In each of those nations, liberty must be won anew in every generation. Thus, most nations most of the time have been authoritarian. In our own day, both modern ideology and modern technology have permitted a large number of authoritarian nations to take radically new steps in the direction of repression and to become totalitarian. This is a phenomenon without precedent.

Totalitarianism is a form of politics compatible with certain intellectual traditions and political concepts, but not with others. In this sense, as Hannah Arendt has explained in *The Origins of Totalitarianism*, totalitarianism is a specific product of a specifically modern ideology. Modern technology has created instruments of repression perfectly suited to this modern ideology.

By pretending not to notice the quantum leap between authoritarian states and totalitarian states—by arguing that we cannot do much, in any case, to change the nature of totalitarian states—the Carter administration tremendously falsified the meaning of human rights. Human rights are incompatible with totalitarian states. The only way to insist upon the existence of human rights is to insist upon institutional changes within totalitarian societies. In an important sense, to declare a worldwide campaign of human rights is to enter into a profound conflict of ideas with totalitarian states. It is seriously to involve oneself in their internal institutional structures. Senator Jackson and Senator Moynihan have clearly understood this. President Carter and his State Department did not. It thus seems plain that what the State Department and the Carter administration meant by human rights is not in fact human rights but only a facsimile thereof. They are like the attendant who whitens the outside of the sepulchre without daring to look within, where the thieves are.

Establishing a Viable Human Rights Policy

JEANE J. KIRKPATRICK

In this paper I deal with three broad subjects:

- First, the content and consequences of the Carter administration's human rights policy;
- Second, the prerequisites of a more adequate theory of human rights;
- And third, some characteristics of a more successful human rights policy.

The Carter Human Rights Policy

How the Carter administration came to be outspokenly committed to the cause of human rights is far from clear. As Daniel Patrick Moynihan has observed, "Human rights as an issue in foreign policy was by no means central to Jimmy Carter's campaign for the presidency. It was raised in the Democratic platform drafting committee, and at the Democratic Convention, but in each instance the Carter representatives were at best neutral, giving the impression of not having heard very much of the matter before and not having any particular views." Indeed, some of candidate Carter's remarks suggested that he was far from wedded to an activist human rights policy. "Our people have now learned," he told the Foreign Policy Association in June 1976, "the folly of our trying to inject our power into the internal affairs of other nations."

Nevertheless, by the time of his inaugural address, Jimmy Carter had become adamant on the subject of human rights. "Our com-

NOTE: This paper was prepared by Ambassador Jeane J. Kirkpatrick, United States permanent representative to the United Nations, for Kenyon College's Human Rights Conference, April 4, 1981. Reprinted from *World Affairs*, 143 (Spring 1981), pp. 323–34, by permission.

mitment to human rights," the new president informed the nation, "must be absolute." Within weeks of his inauguration, President Carter replied to a letter from Andrei Sakharov, and met with the noted Soviet dissident Vladimir Bukovsky in the White House. These symbolic acts generated a great deal of excitement, yet they hardly constituted a human rights policy. On April 30, 1977, however, Secretary of State Vance delivered a major policy address in which he set out to explain just what it was the Carter administration meant by "human rights" and how it intended to promote them. According to Vance, by "human rights" the administration meant three things:

1. The right to be free from governmental violation of the integrity of the person. Such violations include torture; cruel, inhuman, or degrading treatment or punishment; and arbitrary arrest or imprisonment. And they include denial of fair public trial and invasion of the home.

2. The right to the fulfillment of such vital needs as food, shelter, health care, and education. We recognize that the fulfillment of this right will depend, in part, upon the stage of a nation's economic development. But we also know that this right can be violated by a government's action or inaction—for example, through corrupt official processes which divert resources to an elite at the expense of the needy or through indifference to the plight of the poor.

3. The right to enjoy civil and political liberties: freedom of thought, of religion, of assembly; freedom of speech; freedom of the press; freedom of movement both within and outside one's own country; freedom to take part in government.

U.S. policy, Vance stated, "is to promote all these rights." "If we are determined to act," he continued, "the means available range from quiet diplomacy in its many forms, through public pronouncements, to withholding of assistance." Significantly, nowhere in his speech did Vance indicate that human rights rest on specific institutions and that, where these institutions do not exist, neither quiet diplomacy nor public pronouncements nor the withholding of assistance can conjure human rights into being.

In accepting the notion that economic and social "rights" are just as important as civil and political rights, Secretary Vance went well beyond any previous U.S. understanding of human rights. Another prominent administration spokesman on human rights, U.N. Ambassador Andrew Young, went further still. "For most of the world," Young declared, "civil and political rights. . .come as luxuries that are far away in the future." Young called on the U.S. to recognize that there are various equally valid concepts of human rights in the world.

The Soviets, for example, "have...developed a completely different concept of human rights. For them, human rights are essentially not civil and political but economic...."

President Carter, meanwhile, was busy trying to erase the impression, resulting from his letter to Sakharov and his meeting with Bukovsky, that his advocacy of human rights implied an anti-Soviet bias. "I have never had an inclination to single out the Soviet Union as the only place where human rights are being abridged," he told a press conference on February 23, 1977. "I've tried to make sure that the world knows that we're not singling out the Soviet Union for criticism," he again told a press conference on March 24. "I've never made the first comment that personally criticized General Secretary Brezhnev," he told a press conference on June 13. In fact, so eager was the Carter administration not to single out the Soviet Union for criticism that, within a year of its coming into office, Secretary Vance privately instructed the U.S. ambassador to the U.N. Human Rights Commission that under no circumstances was he even to mention the name of the recently arrested Soviet dissident Yuri Orlov.

President Carter's disinclination to single out the Soviet Union for criticism extended to a number of other communist regimes, as well. On April 12, 1978, for example, President Carter informed President Ceausescu of Rumania that "our goals are also the same, to have a just system of economics and politics, to let the people of the world share in growth, in peace, in personal freedom." And on March 4, 1978, in greeting President Tito of Yugoslavia, Carter said, "Perhaps as much as any other person, he exemplifies in Yugoslavia the eagerness for freedom, independence, and liberty that exists throughout Eastern Europe and indeed throughout the world."

But while the Carter administration was notably unwilling to criticize communist states for their human rights violations—not until April 21, 1978, did the administration denounce Cambodia for its massive human rights violations, despite the fact that it had known of these violations for quite some time—it showed no similar reticence when it came to criticizing authoritarian recipients of U.S. aid. In 1976, before the Carter administration came into office, Congress had passed an amendment to the Foreign Assistance Act which, inter alia, required the State Department to submit annual reports to Congress describing the human rights performance of states receiving U.S. aid, and which prohibited the U.S. from assisting states which consistently violated the human rights of their citizens unless the president "certifies in writing that extraordinary circumstances exist." On the basis of the annual reports required by the 1976 law, the Carter administration withheld economic credits and military assistance to Chile, Argentina, Paraguay, Brazil, Nicaragua, and El Salvador. South Korea and the

Philippines continued to receive U.S. aid, on the president's recommendation that such aid served the security interests of the U.S. Nonetheless, the public criticism of those governments helped delegitimize them, at the same time it rendered them *less* susceptible to our views.

These tendencies were exacerbated by the nearly exclusive focus of Carter doctrine and policymakers on violations of human rights by governments. By definition, activities of terrorists and guerrillas could not qualify as violations of human rights, whereas a government's efforts to repress terrorism would quickly run afoul of Carter human rights standards.

This focus not only permitted Carter policy makers to focus on government "repression" while ignoring guerrilla violence, it encouraged consideration of human rights violations independently of context.

Various major actions undertaken by the Carter administration appear to have been derived, either in whole or in part, from its "absolute" commitment to human rights: President Carter's decision, in 1977, to press for ratification of the U.N. Covenants on Economic, Social and Cultural Rights and on Civil and Political Rights; the 1977 decision to support the mandatory U.N. arms embargo against South Africa; the decision, during President Carter's official visit to South Korea in mid-1979, to present the South Korean foreign minister with a privately compiled list of the names of over 100 alleged South Korean political prisoners; Secretary Vance's call, before a meeting of the Organization of American States in June 1979, for the departure of Nicaragua's President Somoza; the decision, in 1979, to withhold U.S. support for the Shah of Iran; and President Carter's decision, in June 1979, not to lift economic sanctions against the Muzorewa government in Zimbabwe Rhodesia.

Viewing the Carter administration's human rights policy in retrospect, it seems fair to conclude that its principal aims were to infuse U.S. foreign policy with "moral content," to create a broad domestic consensus behind the administration's foreign policy goals, and, generally speaking, to make Americans feel good about themselves. Whether the policy succeeded in achieving any of these objectives is debatable. One thing, however, is clear: the thrust of U.S. human rights policy, as it evolved under the Carter administration, was directed against U.S. allies. Instead of using the human rights issue to place the totalitarian states on the defensive, the U.S. frequently joined the totalitarians in attacking pro-Western authoritarian states, and actually helped to destabilize pro-Western regimes in Nicaragua and Iran.

Universal in its rhetoric ("I've worked day and night to make sure that a concern for human rights is woven through everything our government does, both at home and abroad."—Jimmy Carter, 15 December 1977), but almost invariably anti-Western in its application, the Carter human rights policy alienated nondemocratic but friendly nations, enabled anti-Western opposition groups to come to power in Iran and Nicaragua, and reduced American influence throughout the world.

Toward a More Adequate Conception of Human Rights

It is always necessary to know what one is talking about. Although debate about the existential and cognitive status of human rights has occupied philosophical giants in past centuries, recent discussions could profit from renewed and systematic attention to some fundamental distinctions. Four of these seem to me crucial. They are:

- first distinction: between ideas and institutions;
- second distinction: between rights and goals;
- third distinction: between intentions and consequences;
- fourth distinction: between morals and politics.

Ideas and Institutions. There are several important reasons that, in thinking about "rights" (as about all other plans for social systems), it is important to bear in mind the differences between ideas and institutions. Ideas are the product of the mind. They are abstractions which may have no empirical referents. Anything is possible in the domain of abstract reason that does not violate analytical canons which are themselves the products of mind. Robert Owen, for example, proposed "a world convention to emancipate the human race from ignorance, poverty, division, sin, and misery." In our times we propose declarations and laws to attempt to hold other nations responsible for the disappearance of some of these evils to which Owen referred.

Since the world has not arrived at Hegel's promised end where the rational becomes the real and the real rational, there exists no experience with the realization of abstract ideas in society. Many ideas can probably never be realized. Not everything that can be conceived can be created. One can, for example, conceive a unicorn, describe it, destroy whole forests in a determined effort to find one, and still fail. Ideas are readily brought into being and are readily manipulable by their creators. They are susceptible to being changed merely because a decision is made to change them. Their relationship to context is therefore also manipulable—subject to being held constant or altered depending on the decision of their creators.

88

But institutions have very different characteristics. Institutions are stabilized patterns of human behavior. They involve millions, they rest on *expectations* shaped by experience—or they rest on habit and internalized values and beliefs—or on coercion.

These internalized expectations become inextricably bound up with identity. They are extremely resistant to change. Since institutions exist not in the minds of philosophers but in the habits and beliefs of actual people, they can be brought into existence only as people are persuaded or coerced into conforming their thoughts, preferences, and behavior to the necessary patterns. History and recent experience indicate that some kinds of goals and plans cannot finally be implemented, no matter how much persuasion or coercion is employed. Moreover, in the absence of experience there is no way to estimate accurately the feasibility, the costs, even the concrete desirability of an idea or ideal.

Therefore, though rights are easy to claim, they are extremely difficult to translate into reality. In actual societies, unlike in definitions, political principles do not exist in isolation; they interact and the effort at maximization begins at some point to undermine some other value. Frequently the relations among values are themselves embedded in tradition and habit, and profoundly resistant to alteration.

Burke focused on the distinction between ideas and institutions. He said, therefore, of the French Revolution:

> I should therefore suspend my congratulations on the liberty of France until I was informed as to how it had been combined with government, with public force, with discipline, with obedience of armies, with the collection and effectiveness of a well distributed revenue, with morality and religion, with solidity and property, with peace and order, with civil and social manners. All these are good things, too. Without them liberty is of no benefit whilst it lasts and is not likely long to continue.

The failure to distinguish between the domains of rhetoric and politics is the essence of *rationalism*—which encourages us to believe anything that can be conceived can be realized. Rationalism not only encourages utopianism, utopianism is a form of rationalism. It shares the characteristic features, including a disregard of the experience, the concrete probability, in favor of the affirmation of rationality, abstraction, and possibility.

Applied to human rights and foreign policy, disregard of the distinction between ideas and institutions leads to an expectation that declarations of rights have existential status—and constitute valid, practical programs of action.

89

Rights and Goals. The second distinction I want to emphasize is that between rights and goals. In our times, "rights" proliferate at the rhetorical level, with extraordinary speed. To the rights to life, liberty, and security of person have been added the rights to nationality, to privacy, to equal rights in marriage, to education, to culture, to the full development of personality, to self-determination, to self-government, to adequate standards of living.

The United Nations Universal Declaration of Human Rights claims as a universal every political, economic, social right yet conceived.

The Declaration consists of a Preamble and thirty articles, setting forth the human rights and fundamental freedoms to which all men and women, everywhere in the world, are entitled, without any discrimination. Article 1, which lays down the philosophy upon which the Declaration is based, reads: "All human beings are born free and equal in dignity and rights. They are endowed with reason and conscience and should act towards one another in a spirit of brotherhood." Article 2, which sets out the basic principle of equality and nondiscrimination as regards the enjoyment of human rights and fundamental freedoms, forbids "distinction of any kind, such as race, color, sect, language, religion, political or other opinion, national or social origin, property, birth, or other status."

Article 3, a cornerstone of the Declaration, proclaims the right to life, liberty, and security of person: rights which are essential to the enjoyment of all other rights. It introduces the series of articles (4 to 21) in which the human rights of every individual are elaborated further.

The civil and political rights recognized in Articles 4 to 21 of the Declaration include: the right to life, liberty, and security of person; freedom from slavery and servitude; freedom from torture or cruel, inhuman, or degrading treatment or punishment; the right to recognition everywhere as a person before the law; the right to an effective judicial remedy; freedom from arbitrary arrest, detention, or exile; the right to a fair and public hearing by an independent and impartial tribunal; the right to be presumed innocent until proved guilty; freedom from arbitrary interference with privacy, family, home, or correspondence; freedom of movement and residence; the right of asylum; the right to a nationality; the right to marry and found a family; the right to own property; freedom of thought, conscience, and religion; freedom of opinion and expression; the right to peaceful assembly and association; the right of everyone to take part in the government of his country; and the right of everyone to equal access to public service in his country.

Article 22, the second cornerstone of the Declaration, introduces Articles 23 to 27, in which economic, social, and cultural rights—the rights to which everyone is entitled "as a member of society"—are set out. Article 22 reads: "Everyone, as a member of society, has the right to social security and is entitled to realization, through national effort and international cooperation and in accordance with the organization and resources of each state, of the economic, social, and cultural rights indispensable for his dignity and the full development of his personality."

The economic, social, and cultural rights recognized in Articles 23 to 27 include the right to social security, the right to work, the right to equal pay for equal work, the right to leisure, the right to a standard of living adequate for health and well-being, the right to education, and the right to participate in the cultural life of the community.

The concluding articles, Articles 28 to 30, stress that everyone "is entitled to a social and international order in which the rights and freedoms set forth in this Declaration can be fully realized" (Article 28); that "everyone has duties to the community in which alone the free and full development of his personality is possible" (Article 29.1); and that "nothing in this Declaration may be interpreted as implying for any State, group or person any right to engage in any activity aimed at the destruction of any of the rights and freedoms set forth herein."

Recently, in Geneva, the United Nations Commission on Human Rights affirmed a "right to development" which carries its own concomitant list of "rights" including the right to a new economic order, peace, and an end to the arms race.

Such declarations of human "rights" take on the character of "a letter to Santa Claus"—as Orwin and Prangle noted. They can multiply indefinitely because "no clear standard informs them, and no great reflection produced them." For every goal toward which human beings have worked, there is in our time a "right." Neither nature, experience, nor probability informs these lists of "entitlements," which are subject to no constraints except those of the mind and appetite of their authors. The fact that such "entitlements" may be without possibility of realization does not mean they are without consequences.

The consequence of treating goals as rights is grossly misleading about how goals are achieved in real life. "Rights" are vested in persons; "goals" are achieved by the efforts of persons. The language of rights subtly vests the responsibility in some other. When the belief that one has a right to development coincides with facts of primitive technology, hierarchy, and dictatorship, the tendency to blame someone is almost overwhelming. If the people of the world do not fully enjoy their economic rights, it must be because some *one*—some monopoly capitalist, some Zionist, some man—is depriving them of their rightful due.

Utopian expectations concerning the human condition are compounded then by a vague sense that Utopia is one's due; that citizenship in a perfect society is a reasonable expectation for real persons in real societies.

Intentions and Consequences. The third distinction with special relevance to human rights and foreign policy is the distinction between intentions and consequences.

In political philosophy as in ethics there are theories that emphasize motives and those that emphasize consequences.

Preoccupation with motives is a well-known characteristic of a breed of political purist that has multiplied in our times. The distinguishing characteristic of this breed is emphasis on internal criteria, on what one believes and feels is right. Doing what one "knows" is right then becomes more important than producing desired results.

In human rights and foreign policy this position leads to an overweening concern with purity of intentions. When the morality of the motive is more important than the consequences, we are less concerned about creating new traditionalist tyranny than by the morality of our own intentions, and the principal function of a purist policy of human rights is to make us feel good about ourselves.

Personal and Political Morality. The fourth distinction important to thinking about human rights and foreign policy is that between personal and political morality. Where personal morality derives from the characteristics of single individuals and depends on the cultivation of personal virtues such as faith, hope, charity, and discipline, political morality depends on the structured *interactions* of persons—depends, that is, on institutions.

Justice, democracy, liberty are all the products of arrangements of offices and distributions of power. These arrangements and distributions embodied in *constitutions* produce *political* goods by respecting and harmonizing the diverse parts of a political community. The political goods—democracy, due process, protection of "rights" to free speech, assembly—are, as Plato, Aristotle, and the American founding fathers understood, the consequences of wisely structured constitutions.

Rights, then, are embodied in institutions—not rhetoric. They are the consequences of prudential judgments, not good motives. They are always complex and rest on patterns of social life, not on individual virtues.

The consequences of trying to base a human rights policy on private virtue is failure. Where institutions are not constructed on the basis of human proclivities and habits, failure is the inevitable result.

92

Toward a More Successful Human Rights Policy

Human rights can be, should be, must be, will be, taken into account by U.S foreign policy, but we have had enough of rationalism and purism, of private virtues and public vices.

It is my hope that in its approach to human rights, the Reagan administration will take the "cure of history," which is nothing more or less than the cure of reality. If we take the cure of history, we will discover much about the very essence of freedom and the very essence of human rights. We will discover, for example, that the freedom of the American people was based not on the marvelous and inspiring slogans of Thomas Paine but on the careful web of restraint and permission and interests and traditions which was woven by our founding fathers into the Constitution and explained in the Federalist Papers—and rooted, of course, ultimately in our rights as Englishmen. We will find the freedoms of modern France are built not on the slogans of the French Revolution but on the long, arduous struggles of the French people to give reality to these slogans, a reality that exists in the constitutional structures and in the conventions and the institutions of French society.

And adequate human rights policy will also have a realistic conception of the relationships among force, freedom, morality, and power, because history teaches us too that in the real world force may be necessary to reinforce freedom; and today American power is necessary to protect and expand the frontiers of freedom in our time.

We think that by trying less we can produce more. Time, of course, will tell.

How to Keep
Human Rights Alive

EDWARD A. OLSEN

Since the rejection of Ernest Lefever as United States assistant secretary of state for humanitarian affairs, the task of coordinating the administration's human rights policies has been in limbo. Much speculation focuses on the fate of the human rights bureau. Why not revamp it, bring the bureau into conformity with traditional Republican commitments to freedom and liberty at home and abroad?

In order to recast the bureau the administration first must recognize why President Carter's human rights notions got U.S. foreign policy into trouble. Most Americans acknowledge that Carter's human rights failures were byproducts of well-meaning but ill-conceived policies. The Carter administration encouraged progressive change in many countries, but, once "change" began, Carter had no way of limiting or channelling it.

Though there was some excess enthusiasm under Carter, it was not the moral fervor of the American commitment to human rights that caused Washington's problems. Difficulties arose only when the administration made human rights standards a criterion for other U.S. policies, trying to use diplomatic leverage in pursuit of human rights goals.

The Reagan administration must come to grips with morality in U.S. foreign policy. It is neither necessary nor desirable to posit an amoral policy framework. If either friend or foe received the impression that Washington was abandoning its moral principles, this would imperil U.S. national interests.

However, the U.S. should keep its moral principles in proper perspective. Moral ideals always should be seen as "ideals," not absolute criteria against which policy is measured. With rare exceptions, moral principles are poor coercive mechanisms in U.S. foreign policy.

A revamped human rights office under President Reagan should be made less subjective, less politicized, and less policy-oriented by:

• Concentrating on minimum standards to which no reasonable people could object (i.e., on torture, slavery, genocide, minimal jurisprudence, etc.);

• Measuring, in a uniform and objective manner, the performance of every state in the international system, regardless of its stature or influence;

• Making no attempt to impose these standards on the nations of the world or on U.S. policy towards those nations.

Such a new mandate for the human rights office would strip it of any veto power over the policy recommendations of the regional or functional bureaus at the State Department. The power of human rights "clearance" under Carter led to an enormous waste of time, money, and effort. It also strengthened the voice of human rights activists. The combination of "clearance" and a noisy constituency produced more bureaucratic clout than the bureau deserved. All this could be reduced sharply by revamping the human rights office.

A revitalized human rights bureau should be more objective and more credible as an officially sanctioned guide to global conditions. This would allow Washington to retain a vehicle for upholding American moral goals in the international arena without intervening in the affairs of other states.

The U.S. still could proclaim its ideals for the world to examine. If it lives in accordance with its ideals, it can hope others will see it as an example to emulate. When most choose not to conform to what Americans see as minimal standards of behavior, they can tell the world where they think violations exist and how severe they are.

But, by not trying to use political or economic leverage to compel change in countries that violate such standards, the U.S. frees itself from two liabilities. First, it will not aggravate instability in its client states. If they are going to fail internally and as an American ally, let it be their fault, not America's. Second, the U.S. would not have to contend with guilty states flaunting their violations in the face of its human rights–burdened foreign policy, clearly exposing U.S. inability to effect change.

Far from abdicating America's moral standards, this proposal would prove more effective by measuring every state on an equitable basis. This would be possible precisely because the revamped human rights bureau would not have to clear its judgments with any policy bureau. Its judgments would be independent and informational, not explicitly linked to policy considerations. This would free the Department of State from the rancorous infighting which inhibited both policymakers and human rights officials under Carter, making neither as effective as they might have been.

Selected AEI Publications